John Bull in America

James Kirke Paulding

LITERATURE HOUSE / GREGG PRESS
Upper Saddle River, N. J.

Republished in 1970 by
LITERATURE HOUSE
an imprint of The Gregg Press
121 Pleasant Avenue
Upper Saddle River, N. J. 07458

Reprinted from original edition in
Rare Book Collection
Rutgers University

Standard Book Number–8398-1554-9
Library of Congress Card–71-104536

77- 9965
Printed in United States of America

JOHN BULL IN AMERICA;

OR,

THE NEW MUNCHAUSEN.

NEW-YORK:

CHARLES WILEY, No. 3 WALL-STREET

G. F. HOPKINS, PRINTER.

. . . . . .

1825.

PREFACE OF THE EDITOR.

On the fifth day of August, 1824, a rather genteel looking stranger arrived at the Mansion Hotel in the city of Washington, where he inquired
for a retired room, and expressed his intention of
staying some time. He was dressed in a blue frock,
striped vest, and gray pantaloons; was about five
feet ten, as is supposed, and had a nose like a potato. The evening of the following day there arrived in the stage from Baltimore, a little mahogany-faced foreigner, a Frenchman as it would seem,
with gold rings in his ears, and a pair of dimity
breeches. The little man in dimity breeches expressed great pleasure at meeting the stranger, with
whom he seemed tò be well acquainted; but the
stranger appeared much agitated at the rencontre,
and displayed nothing like satisfaction on the occasion. With the evident intention of avoiding the
little dark complexioned man, he, in a few minutes,

desired the waiter to show him into his room, to
which he retired without bidding the other good
night.

It appears from the testimony of the waiter, that
on going into his chamber, and observing a portmanteau, which had been placed there in his absence, the stranger inquired to whom it belonged
The waiter replied: " to the French gentleman
As you seemed to be old acquaintance, I thought
you would like to be together, sir." This information seemed to cause great agitation in the mind
of the stranger, who exclaimed, as if unconscious
of the presence of the waiter, "I am a lost man!"
which the waiter thought rather particular. The
stranger, after a few moments apparent perplexity,
ordered the waiter to bring him pen, ink, paper,
and sealing-wax, and then desired to be left alone.
It is recollected that the dark complexioned foreigner retired about ten, requesting to be called
up at four o'clock, as he was going on in the stage
to the south. This is the last that was seen, either
of the stranger, or the dark-complexioned foreigner. On knocking at the door precisely at four
o'clock the next morning, and no answer being
given, the waiter made bold to enter the room,
which to his surprise he found entirely empty.
Neither trunks nor stranger, nor dark complexioned foreigner, were to be found. Had the stranger and his friend previously run up a long score
at the Mansion Hotel, their disappearance would
not have excited any extraordinary degree of sur-

prise. But the stranger was indebted but for two
days board and lodging, and the dark complexioned foreigner had paid his bill over night. A person who slept in the next room, recollected hearing a stir in that of the stranger, as he thinks, about
three o'clock, but supposing it to be some one going off in the mail, it excited no particular observation.

This is all that could be gathered in relation to
the mysterious disappearance of these two travellers. But on searching about the room a packet
was found carefully sealed, and directed " To the
Editor of the —— ;" the rest was wanting, and the
omission was probably occasioned by some circumstance occurring at the instant, which led to the
singular affair above detailed. Some days having
elapsed without any thing occurring to throw light
on the transaction, it was thought proper to open
the packet, the direction of which afforded no clue
by which to transmit it to the persons intended, in
the hope that something might be learned from it,
that would lead to a discovery of the names, or the
friends of these mysterious persons. On inspec-
tion it proved to be a manuscript of travels in the
United States, of which the following is a faithful
transcript. Though, as the reader will perceive,
it explains very satisfactorily the principal portion
of the preceding details, there was nothing in it
which could lead directly to a discovery of the
name and residence of the unfortunate gentleman
whose fate, although still enveloped in doubt, is

but too easily anticipated. All that appears certain from the manuscript, is that the stranger was
an Englishman, travelling to New-Orleans on business, and that he probably was in some way mys-
teriously made away with by the little dark complexioned foreigner, of whom a description has
been given, and for whom a reward has been offered in the public papers without effect. His
name, as given by himself, in the examination before the magistrate in New-York is probably fic-
titious.

After mature reflection, it was decided to publish the manuscript, as the best and cheapest mode
of extending the inquiry concerning the identity
of this unfortunate stranger to all parts of the reading world, and thereby acquiring further information. In addition to this motive it was thought
that a work of such extraordinary merit as to style,
sentiment, and accuracy of detail, deserved to be
made known. Much discussion took place in respect to the selection of a title for the work, which
had been omitted in the manuscript. To announce
it simply as a book of travels in America, would
have been to place it on a footing with the various
romances which have been published under that
title within the last thirty years. Of these we
have lately had such a profusion that the public is
rather tired, as we are informed by the booksellers.
Some familiar and striking title-page, no matter
whether applicable or not to the character of the
work, was therefore necessary to excite public at-

tention, and it was finally decided to adopt that
which appears, and which we will now proceed
to explain.

The character of these travels being that of severe and inflexible truth, a title was chosen in direct antithesis, partly in a sportive imitation of the
facetious philosopher Lucian, who gave the name
of "a true story" to one of the most improbable
fictions of antiquity; and partly in allusion to Dr.
Jonathan Swift, who in like manner disguised one
of the gravest of satires, under the mask of "A
Tale of a Tub," than which nothing can be more
opposite to its real character. Thus, in like manner, have we availed ourselves of the catachresis
on this occasion, not only for the purpose of agreeably surprising the reader into the perusal of a
work of incomparable veracity, under the garb of
a work of fiction, but also to administer to the public taste, which, owing to the witcheries of that
mischievous person called the "Great Unknown,"
hath an unseemly propensity towards romances
and the like.

In this we are justified, not only by the foregoing high authorities, but in an especial manner by
the example of certain great critics, who place at
the head of their articles, by way of title-page,
the name of a book about which they say not one
word in the whole course of their lucubrations.
So, in like manner, may we see certain well-mean-
ing and orthodox writers, publishing what they
call "candid examinations," and "cool consider-

ations," of and concerning certain disputed points,
which, to say the truth, are neither candid nor
cool, but marvellously the contrary.   We mention not these things in a spirit of hostility, but to
justify our adoption of the figure of the catachresis by their examples.   The reader will therefore
err most egregiously if he supposes for a moment
that the following work, whatever be its title, bears
the most remote resemblance, or is in any wise
tainted with the egregious fictions of the genuine
Munchausen.

Touching the real author of this work, whom
we may safely pronounce a second and still greater
"Great Unknown," we have our suspicions on
the subject, suspicions almost amounting to a certainty, which we shall proceed to lay before the
reader.   At first, for divers good reasons, we were
inclined to suppose the author was no less a person
than the "Great Unknown" himself, who as is
asserted, resided in America some time.   But
however rich, redundant, and inexhaustible may
be the invention of this extraordinary Incognito,
no one we think will deny to our author, notwithstanding his general character of severe veracity, a
vigour of fancy and a vein of inventive sportiveness,
vastly superior even to the "Great Unknown."
We must therefore discard this suggestion and proceed to put the reader in possession of our settled
conviction on this matter, which as will be seen
amounts to next to a certainty.

To come to the point without further circumlocution, we have the best reasons as well as the highest circumstantial testimony to warrant us in the assertion, that the author of this work, was, and if living, is still, one of the principal writers of the Quarterly Review—the very person who wrote the masterly review of Faux's Travels in the fifty-eighth number.* To arrive at this conclusion it is only necessary to compare the two works, in the articles of style, temper, and feeling, every thing in short which goes to the indication of a personal identity. The style of this work displays the closest resemblance to that of the article on Mr Faux's Travels, and indeed all the articles relating to the United States, in the Quarterly Review. The same classical severity and mildness of rebuke, where rebuke is necessary—the same happy aptitude in the selection of choice flowers of rhetoric—the same amiable zeal for religion—the same charity to all men—the same principles of universal benevolence—the same gentlemanly observance of the slightest minutiæ of high-wrought and refined good breeding, runs through each and all of these productions. Nay, the same expressions and peculiar phrases which characterize the reviewer, occur almost in every page of our author. We have the "turbulent spirit of democra-

* The reader must consult the English copy for this article, which was so extravagantly complimentary, that even the American bookseller modestly omitted it in his re-publication of the number.

cy"—the "wanton violations of the Sabbath"—
the "total disregard of religion"—the "spitting,
gouging, drinking, duelling, dirking, swearing,
strutting republicans"—the "white-robed, levee
going, cow-hiding fine lady"—the "hog-stealing
judges"—"the illusions of transatlantic speculation"—"the flippant farragoes of impiety, malevolence, folly, and radical trash"—together with an
infinite variety of the favourite phrases of the
Quarterly repeated over and over again, with a
facility,which we think can only be accounted for
on the supposition that the author and reviewer
are one and same person.

Again, a perfect similarity of temper as well as
style reigns throughout both productions. The
same display of candour, good nature, urbanity,
morality, piety, orthodoxy, and loyalty—the
same inflexible impartiality and love of truth—
the same chivalrous gallantry to the ladies—the
same high-toned courtesy to the gentlemen of this
republic—and the same intense horror of the turbulent spirit of democracy, lives, breathes, and moves
in each. It were too great a stretch of credulity,
to suppose that one kingdom, one quarter of the
world, or even the whole universe, could possibly
at one and the same time, contain two persons so
highly and so equally gifted with such extraordinary qualifications. It would be too much for one
age. We read indeed of a young Mede, who assured Cyrus that he had two souls ; but the idea of
two separate persons having one and the same soul,

is altogether preposterous. The author of this work, and the superintendent of American affairs in the Quarterly Review, are therefore manifestly one and the same. This decision acquires additional support from the continual reference to, and quotations from, the latter work, interspersed throughout the whole of the former. It is scarcely possible to believe that any person but the reviewer himself, could so accurately remember and refer to the most admired passages. Our author, indeed, seems never to have had the Quarterly out of mind, and this circumstance, together with the fact of his always carrying it about with him, and reading it on all occasions, is another decisive proof; since we have occasion to know from our own experience, that an author ever prefers his own works to all others, as certainly as a parent does his own children.

Other symptoms of identity occur in almost every page. Both these productions are equally remarkable, for that friendly disposition to the people, the government, and institutions of the United States, which has caused the Quarterly to be so extensively circulated in this country, and patronized by its most distinguished citizens. It would be absurd to suppose that two persons, and those persons foreigners, should at one and the same time be animated by such disinterested feelings of good will towards the people of this, or any other country. We notice, likewise, several other striking similarities; especially an equally accurate knowledge of the geography and history of the United States. The amiable credulity of our author, in occasionallly suffering himself to be imposed upon by the relations of others, is also a characteristic of the reviewer, who it must be confessed sometimes stretches his belief into the regions of the marvellous.— This credulity is joined with a certain engaging simplicity which appears, in occasionally exhibiting himself in a ridiculous light, without appearing to be aware of it, and relating things which a more artful and wary person would pass óver without notice. This we look upon as the strongest proof of his veracity, and a guaranty for the truth of every thing he advances upon his own authority. In regard to what is told him by others, we would advise the reader to receive it with some grains of allowance.

Having thus, as we presume to imagine, pretty clearly established our position, that the author of the following pages, and the writer of American criticisms in the Quarterly, is one and the same person, we shall proceed to indulge in a few speculations as to the precise individual to whom the people of the United States have so frequently been indebted for such friendly notices.

It cannot be the laureat, Mr. Southey, because we are assured he has lately taken rather a dislike to republicans, on account of their blamable indifference to his epic poems. Having in one of these taken the trouble to confer upon them a respectable

degree of dignity and antiquity, by peopling the
country with a colony of Welsh, commanded by a
real prince, with an enormous long pedigree, it
is another proof of the ingratitude of republics, that
the Americans should be so indifferent on the occasion. The Laureat's dislike is, therefore, however much it may be lamented, not to be wondered
at. But besides this, we have occasion to know
that the Laureat finds it such a difficult matter to
do justice to the glories of his present gracious
sovereign, that he has been high and dry aground
upon a birthday ode for the last nine months, and
there is no telling when he will be delivered. It
is whispered in the literary circles, that he has
called for another butt of sack, to float him off.
Others say, that in addition to this, he is engaged
upon a second "Vision of Judgment," in which his
old antagonist, the late Lord Byron, is condemned to a most unheard of punishment, to wit, that of
reading over all the Laureat's epics, sapphics, &c.
not forgetting Wat Tyler, twice a year, till he becomes orthodox, and believes in the divine right
of kings.

Neither do we think it can possibly be Mr.
D'Israeli, it being pretty generally understood
that he is entirely devoted to the ladies, and that
his specified duty is to keep an eye upon Lady
Morgan, to whose " flippant impieties," &c. his
acknowledged orthodoxy is held to be a most sovereign antidote. We remember to have read in the
London Morning Chronicle, (a most mischievous

B

gossipping paper,) if we mistake not, that Mr.
D—— was the author of a certain Review in the
Quarterly, in which like one of Tasso's or Arios-
to's gallant knights, he tilted mortally at our Lady
Errant, not with lance but pen, and demonstrated
to the satisfaction of the world that the good old
Jewish rite had not in the least impaired his man-
hood.

We had at one time settled it in our minds, that
these productions came from the pen of the good
natured creature who has so long presided over
the Quarterly, whereby it hath become so renown-
ed throughout all Christendom, for that refined
and high-wrought courtesy, which is only to be
acquired in the cabin of a Newcastle collier.——
These suspicions were strengthened by our being
credibly informed of a little good-tempered old
gentleman, who was in this country some time
last Spring, and was so delighted with every thing
he saw that he fell seriously ill of an ecstatic trans-
port, from which he was finally recovered by
smelling a bottle of the pure essence of democracy.
These facts staggered us a little; but positive information has since been received that the good
man was at that time confined to his house, No.
68 Grub-street, with a dyspepsy, accompanied by
lowness of spirits, occasioned, as is conjectured,
by the late act of Parliament abolishing lotteries,
whereby his office of comptroller of lottery-offices
naturally falls to the ground.   It is surmised that
the orthodox old gentleman hath it in serious

contemplation to abandon the Quarterly, become
very wicked, and devote himself to democracy and
impiety, unless they bolster up his principles with
another sinecure.*

The reader will doubtless give us due credit,
when we assure him we have reduced it to a probability, approaching very near to certainty, that
the real author of the productions, which have
been the subject of this inquiry, is a gentleman of
great orthodoxy, generally known in England by
the appellation of " THE TALKING POTATO." We
have been at some pains to come at the origin of
this whimsical distinction, but upon the whole
have not succeeded exactly to our wishes. By
some, it is said, it arose from his talking as if he
had a hot potato in his mouth ; by others, that it
came from his having a nose wonderfully resem-
bling the *Solanum Tuberosum,* or red potato.
But the most general opinion is, that it originated
in his once having had the misfortune to require
trepanning, when Sir Astley Cooper, the great
surgeon, was astonished to find the entire cavity of
the brain occupied by a thumping Irish potato.
This fact was communicated to the college of
physicians, but without mentioning the name, and

* Previous to this act, abolishing Lotteries, Mr. G., it is understood, held two sinecures, to wit, that of paymaster to the " Honourable band of Gentlemen Pensioners," and that to which we
have just alluded. The former was given him to support his loyalty, and the latter to maintain his orthodoxy. It is supposed that
either his loyalty or religion will be buried under the ruins of the
lottery offices.

may be found in one of the volumes of their trans-
actions.

This gentleman, besides his holding " something in the nature of a sinecure," is a member
of parliament, and, as we are informed, one of the
genteellest writers of the Quarterly. Besides
all this, he is considered the best joker in the
House, with the exception of Mr. Canning. He
has not the wit of Mr. Canning, but then, as the
country members are wont to say in a debate on
the causes of agricultural distress, while they are
splitting their sides with laughter, " he talks so
like a potato." It is a state secret with which we
have chanced to become possessed, that the " talking potato," did actually come over here sometime in the late recess of Parliament, for the sole
purpose of ascertaining the real causes of various
naval phenomena which occurred during the late
war between England and the United States, a
subject which had excited great curiosity among
my lords of the admiralty. We understand he
ascertained pretty clearly, that the whole secret
lay in the trifling circumstances, of a superiority of
ships, officers, seamen, and gunnery. This discovery put him in such good humour, that he was
wrought upon to compliment the people and country in the polite manner exemplified in the following pages. It is surmised that the result of his mission, in relation to naval matters, will appear in the
next edition of Mr. Robert James's Apology for the
English Navy. With respect to his object in go-

ing to New-Orleans, we have some suspicion that it might have been a part of his mission to account for the wonderful disparity of loss in the great battle between the British and the stout hero of New-Orleans.

The foregoing contains all the particulars we have been able to obtain in elucidation of the following work. We cannot, however, refrain from expressing our earnest hopes, that the doubts of his friends, and the fears of his country in regard to the fate of this unfortunate gentleman, may be speedily removed by his reappearing and claiming this work, to the credit and profits of which he is entirely welcome. Should the contrary be the case, we beg permission to offer our sincere condolements to my lords of the admiralty, to the country members, on the loss of their favourite jester; to the Quarterly Review on the loss of its most classical writer; and to the nation at large on the loss of so useful a person as "The Talking Potato."

Washington, 10th October, 1824.

JOHN BULL IN AMERICA;

OR THE

NEW MUNCHAUSEN.

····»»◉◉◉◉«««····

CHAP. I.

Impressions of the author previous to his arrival in America—
Embarks from Liverpool—Voyage—Sea-serpent—Arrives at
Boston, the capital of the state of Kennebunk—Account of the
city—Manners of the people—Mansion-house hotel, kept by
William Renshaw, an Englishman—Turbulent spirit of democracy—Negroes—-Earthquakes—-Inundations—Intemperance
—Ignorance—-Impudence—-Barbarity-—Athenæum—-Litera-
ture—Naval Officer—Turbulent spirit of democracy—Quarterly Review, &c.—Leave Boston.

PREVIOUS to my departure for the Western
paradise of liberty, my impressions with regard
to the country were, upon the whole, rather of a
favourable character. It is true, I did not believe
a word of the inflated accounts given by certain
French revolutionary travellers, such as Brissot,
Chastellux, and others; much less in those of Birkbeck, Miss Wright, Captain Hall, and the rest of

1

the radical fry. I was too conversant with the
Quarterly Review, to be led astray by these Uto-
pian romancers, and felt pretty well satisfied that
the institutions of the country were altogether
barbarous. I also fully believed that the people
were a bundling, gouging, drinking, spitting, impious race, without either morals, literature, religion, or refinement; and that the turbulent spirit
of democracy was altogether incompatible with any
state of society becoming a civilized nation. Being
thus convinced that their situation was, for the present, deplorable, and in the future entirely hope-
less, unless they presently relieved themselves
from the cumbrous load of liberty, under which
they groaned, I fell into a sort of compassion for
them, such as we feel for condemned criminals,
having no hope of respite, and no claim to benefit
of clergy.

Under this impression, and with a determination
to look to the favourable side of the subject on all
occasions; to be pleased with every thing I saw,
and to make a reasonable allowance for the faults
originating in their unhappy situation, I left England. I can safely lay my hand on my heart, and
declare to the world, that I was, and still am, as
free from prejudice against any nation whatever,
as any English traveller who has ever visited this
country.

Being fully aware of the superiority of British
ships and British sailors, I declined the advice of
certain merchants at Liverpool, to embark in one

of the line of American packets, and took passage
on board the British brig Wellington, for Boston,
as my business was principally in New-Orleans,
and I wished to arrive at the nearest port. I did
not like to go directly for New-Orleans, being
apprehensive of the yellow-fever, which rages there
all the year round, with such virulence that the
people all die off there regularly once in two years.
Our passage was long and tedious, so much so that
the Packet in which I was advised to sail from Liverpool, arrived at Boston four weeks before the Wellington. But this I am assured was owing more
to good fortune than to any superiority either in
the ship or sailors, over those of the mistress of
the seas. I passed my time both pleasantly and
profitably in reading the Quarterly.

On the seventieth day from losing sight of Old
England, we made land at Cape Hatteras, which
forms the eastern point of Boston Bay, which we
entered just before sun-set; and being favoured
with a fine fair wind from the north, came up to
the wharf in about two hours from entering the
Capes. Coming up, we saw the famous sea-serpent, but he was nothing to those I had frequently
seen in the Serpentine, so called from its abound-
ing in these articles. Being very anxious to go on
shore, I desired one of the sailors to call a hack,
which very soon arriving, I ordered the fellow to
drive me to the best hotel in the place : accordingly he put me down at the mansion-house hotel,
kept by William Renshaw, a place of great repu-

tation throughout the United States. The fellow charged me a quarter of a dollar, which is twice as much as I should have paid in London! Being determined not to be imposed upon, I appealed to the landlord, who assured me it was all right; so I paid him, after giving himself and his horses a hearty malediction.

The landlord, civilly enough, considering the country I was in, desired to know if I wished to have a room for the night. I answered him in the affirmative, and begged, as a particular favour, that he would put me into one with not more than six beds in it. He seemed a little surprised, but assured me my wishes should be gratified. I was accordingly shown into a neat room enough, with a single bed. Ay, ay, thought I, this landlord knows how to distinguish his guests—but my wonder subsided when the waiter, who I was surprised to find was a white man, told me his master was an Englishman.

Soon after I was called down to supper, where I found twenty or thirty persons, all perfect strangers to me, and who, seeing I was a stranger I suppose, paid me those little civilities, which, to one who knows the world, are always sufficient to put him on his guard. Accordingly I declined them all, and answered the questions put to me rather short, insomuch that a person, who I took to be a naval officer, seemed inclined to quarrel with me. Nothing indeed can be more disgusting to a stranger than these civilities, from people one

does not know; and nothing gave me a more un-
favourable impression of the rude manners of these
republicans, than the freedom with which they
chatted about their private affairs, and joked each
other before me, a perfect stranger. It displayed
a want of—tact—a familiarity so different from the
conduct of people in similar circumstances in London, that I retired to my room in disgust. I afterwards learned that the naval officer threatened to
" lick" me, as he called it, for my surly ill manners, as he was pleased to denominate my gentlemanly reserve.

I retired to rest, and found my bed tolerable
enough; but the American goose feathers are by no
means as soft as those of London. In the morning
I went down to breakfast, determined to keep
these forward gentry at a distance. But it did not
appear to be necessary, as none of these rude boors
took the least notice of me, and if I wanted any
thing, I was obliged to call the waiter to bring it
to me, for no one offered to hand it about the table;
I was exceedingly disgusted at this Gothic want of
politeness, which, however, was nothing strange,
considering the vulgar habits of equality which pre-
vail in this republic; so I called for a coach, with
an air of importance, and rode round the city, with
a view of seeing into the character and habits of
the people.

The first thing that struck me, was the vast dis-
proportion of negroes, in the streets and every
where else. I may affirm, with perfect veracity,

that nearly one half the inhabitants of Boston are black.   Each of these poor creatures has a white man always standing over him, with a large club about the thickness of a man's arm, with which he beats the poor slave for his amusement.   I assure you I have seen, I may say, a thousand instances of this kind of a morning.   There is hardly a slave here that has not his head covered with scars, and bound up with a handkerchief; and almost every step you take, you perceive the stains of blood upon the pavement, which, I am assured by Governor Hancock himself, is that of the negroes.   I have seen a lady of the first distinction here, walking the Mall, as it is called, with a stout black-fellow behind her, and occasionally amusing herself with turning round and scratching his face till it was covered with blood.   This *Mall* is a place of about half an acre, covered with dust, with a few rotten elms, and a puddle in the centre.   Even the little children here are initiated into human blood almost as soon as they are able to walk; and the common amusement of young persons is to stick pins in their black attendants, while every boy has a little negro, of about his own age, to torture for his pastime.

The blacks here, as I was assured by his excellency the Governor, whose name is Hancock, have but one meal a day, which is principally potatoes, and fare little better than the miserable Irish or English peasantry at home.   The Governor told me a story of a man, who tied his black servant naked to a stake, in one of the neighbouring cane-brakes, near the city, which abound with a race of moschetoes that bite through a boot. Here he was left one night, in the month of December, which is a spring month in this climate, and the next morning was found stone dead, without a drop of blood in his body. I asked if this brutal tyrant was not brought to justice? The Governor shrugged up his shoulders and replied, that he was now a member of Congress!

To an Englishman, who is only accustomed to see white men in a state of slavery and want, it is shocking to see black ones in a similar situation. My heart bled, with sympathy for the wrongs of this injured race, and I could not sufficiently admire the philanthropy of the members of the Holy alliance, who have lately displayed such a laudable compassion for the blacks.

Next to the continual recurrence of these disgusting exhibitions of cruelty, the most common objects seen in the streets of Boston, are drunken men, women, and children. I was assured by the Mayor, Mr. Phillips, one of the most charitable and philanthropic men in the State of Maine, that on an average, every third person was drunk every day, by nine o'clock in the morning. The women however, don't get fuddled, he tells me, till after they have cleared the breakfast table, and put the room to rights, when they set to and make merry with the young children, not one in a hundred of whom ever see the inside of a school, or a church.

The consequences of this mode of life are, that the whole of the people exhibit a ruddy complexion, and what appears at first sight to be a strong muscular figure; but on a closer examination the roses will be found to be nothing more than what is called grog-blossoms, and the muscular appearance only bloated intemperance.

Ignorance is the natural result of a want of knowledge, as the Quarterly says. Consequently, where children never go to school, it is not probable that learning will flourish. Accordingly, nothing can equal the barbarous ignorance of both the children and grown up persons in this republican city. I happened to be at the house of a judge of one of the courts, and was astonished to find, on my giving his son, a boy of about twelve years old, a book to read, that he could not comprehend a single word! The poor mother, who was, I suppose, a little mortified on account of my being a stranger, (they don't mind these things among themselves,) patted the booby on the back, and assured me the poor boy was *so* bashful! Most of the justices of the peace here, make their mark, instead of signing their names to warrants, &c. and what is difficult to believe, many of the clerks in the banks can't write their names. I never saw a school while in Boston. There is a college, to be sure, but I was assured the professors did not quite understand English. The Rev. Cotton Mather, one of the most enlightened and popular preachers here, has written a book called the Magnalia, in which he gives a variety of witch stories, such as would be laughed at, even among the Indians, but which they all believe here, as if it were Holy Writ. The work is just come out, and affords apt illustration of the state of the human intellect on this side of the Atlantic.

Religion is, if possible, in a worse state than literature, manners, or morals. There is not a single church in Boston, nor any religious exercises on Sunday, except in a few *school rooms*, by the methodists and other fanatics. I am assured it is the custom all over New-England, as well as in the states of Newburyport and Pasquotank, to spend the Sabbath like every other day in the week, except that they put on clean clothes, a thing never thought of, even among the most fashionable ladies, except on that occasion.

Boston is a terrible place for fevers and agues. Every one of the inhabitants, except the slaves, is afflicted with them in the spring and autumn, as sure as the leaves appear in the former, and fall in the latter. The consequence is, that they look like so many ghosts, without flesh or blood, and if you go into the shops, you may hear the money jingling in the pockets of the shop-keepers, by the mere force of habit, even if the poor man should happen, at that moment, to be free from the ague; or "shake," as they call it.

Besides this, they have earthquakes and inundations, three times a week if not more. After the earthquake generally comes an inundation, which destroys all the crops for hundreds of miles round, and covers the country so, that the tops of trees and chimneys just appear above the water.   This is succeeded by a fog so thick, that many persons are lost in the streets of Boston, and wander about several days, without being able to find any of the houses.   This is the origin of the phrase " I guess," so universal in New-England; for these fogs are so common, that one half the time people are obliged to " guess" at what they are about.   Hence, too, the half pint of whiskey which every man takes in the morning the first thing he does after getting up, is called an anti-fogmatic.

These are the principal things I observed in my morning's ride.   At dinner the naval officer took occasion to make himself most indecently merry, with certain sarcasms on the stupid, surly, self-importance, which *some* people attempted to pass off for real dignity and high breeding.   The rudeness of republicanism, indeed, is obvious to the most superficial observer from the first moment a man sets foot in this country of beastly equality. After dinner a person who had been troubling me with his attentions, since my arrival, offered to carry me to the Athenæum, a great literary institution, where they read newspapers, and talk politics, which they mistake for literature.   I must not forget to observe, that nothing can be worse than the taste of these people, which is perfectly barbarous, except their genius, which is perfectly barren.

Nothing is read here but newspapers, almanacs, dying-speeches, ghost stories, and the like. Their greatest scholar is Noah Webster, who compiled a spelling-book, and their greatest poet the author of Yankee doodle. The utmost effort of republican genius is to write an additional stanza to this famous song, which, in consequence of these perpetual contributions, is, by this time, almost as long as a certain Persian poem, which, if I recollect right, consisted of one hundred and twenty thousand verses.

I brought letters to some of the principal magnificoes here, but did not deliver them. I like the dinners and old wine of these vulgarians, but really it is paying too much for them to be obliged to listen to their vulgar hemp, cotton, tobacco, and nankeen speculations, without being allowed the privilege of laughing, or even yawning in their stupid faces. Then one is obliged to drink wine with madam, be civil to her dowdy daughters, who " guess they have no occasion for dancing"---and what is the climax of horrors, retire from the dinner-table to the drawing-room, to hear miss break the sixth commandment in the matter of half a dozen sonatas, and two dozen of Moore's Melodies.

By the time I had sojourned a single day in the land of promise, I began to be mortally ennuyé. I inquired of the waiter if there was any thing in the *fancy* way going on. He replied there were plenty of fancy stores in Court-street!—I asked if there was likely to be a mob soon, as I had heard these

republicans amused themselves in that way. He
replied, that mobs never happened in Boston.
Any executions? No—" My G—d," exclaimed
I in despair, " what a dull place!" I devoted the
evening to packing up, and after supper, being desirous to make an impression on these bumpkin
demos, called out loudly to the waiter, in my best
Corinthian tone—" Waiter!—you infernal waiter!" " Here, sir." " Waiter, bring a boot-jack
and pair of slippers." " Waiter—you infernal
waiter," replied a voice which I took for an echo.
" Here, sir," said the waiter. " Waiter, bring
me two boot-jacks, and two pair of slippers." On
looking round I perceived the echo was my old
enemy, the naval officer. Being determined, however, to take no notice of such a low fellow, I again
called out.—" Waiter, bring a candle into my
chamber, and a warming pan to warm my bed."—
" Waiter, bring two candles, and two warming-
pans, into my chamber. I shall sleep in two beds
to night," cried echo. I gave him a look of withering contempt and walked out of the room, leaving behind me a horse laugh, which, as I judged,
proceeded from these illiterate cyclops. Before I
went to bed I looked over the fifty-eighth num
ber of the Quarterly to refresh my memory.

CHAP. II.

BEING determined to hold as little communica-
tion as possible with the turbulent spirit of democracy, the next day, without asking any questions,
I took the stage, crossed a bridge to the north of
Boston, which bestrides the Potomac river, and in
less than half an hour arrived in Charleston, the
capital of the state of North Carolina, a city famous
for eating negroes. It is about three miles from
Boston. There is a navy-yard at this place which
I visited, and saw a ship building there which is
four hundred and twenty yards long, and as Capt.
Hull, the commandant, assured me, would carry

three hundred long forty-two pounders. She is called a seventy-four! The captain, who is a tall rough-looking man, with black eyes and immense whiskers, told me in confidence, that the only way he could persuade the yankee sailors to stand to their guns in his engagement with the gallant Dacres, was by promising them, in case of victory, to roast the fat black cook of the Constellation, as his ship was called, for supper. Nothing will make these cannibal republicans fight like a temptation of this sort.

Charleston is about the size of Boston, but has neither pavements nor sidewalks, and alternates between mud and dust, and dust and mud. In summer it is all dust, in winter all mud. Indeed I began to perceive, the moment I arrived here, that I had got amongst a different sort of people from those of Boston. There was no one to be seen in the streets but negroes stark naked as they were born, with their backs striped like a leopard in consequence of the frequent application of the lash. In fact, the principal article for sale here at the retail shops, is the cow-hide, as it is called, that is, a hard ox skin, twisted in the shape of a whip. Almost every man you see has one of these in his hand, and a spur at his heel, to make people believe he carries the whip for his horse. But I was assured by the head waiter at the city hotel, kept by Mr. Chester Jennings, in Charleston, that it was for the purpose of beating the slaves. Nothing indeed will tempt the whites to exert themselves in this enervating climate, but the luxury " of licking a fellow," as they call it, and almost the first thing I noticed in coming into the city, was a tall, lank, cadaverous figure, strutting up and down, cutting and hacking with his cow-hide at every negro man, woman, and child, that came in his way. I inquired of the driver what these blacks had been guilty of. " Guilty," replied he, " guilty—eh! —O, lord bless you sir, it's only Judge D—— amusing himself with the niggers." It made my heart bleed to see the blood running down their backs. It was almost as bad as shooting the Irish peasants for being out after nine o'clock.

I had scarcely been at my hotel an hour when this same Judge D—— called upon me, as a stranger, and invited me to dinner the next day. My blood rose up against the brute, but as I wished to see whether some of the stories told about these people, and which they deny, were true, I accepted his invitation. The party consisted of Judge D——'s wife, two daughters, and about a dozen of the principal men of the place, among whom was the governor of South-Carolina, Mr. Heister. Behind each of the seats, as well the judge's as those of his lady, and daughters, stood a black boy or girl, as it happened, perfectly naked, and each of the guests were provided with a cow-hide, with which to chastise any neglect of duty on the part of the slaves. There was cut and come again. The judge and his guests cut their meat and cut the negroes *ad interim,* and I particularly noticed the

dexterity of the young ladies in touching the ten-
der places with the cow-hide, as well as their infinite delight in seeing them wince under the application.   One of these poor wretches having the
misfortune to break a plate during dinner, was
taken out, put under the window by the overseer,
and beat so cruelly that her moans were heard
over half the city.   When she came in again, the
tears were rolling down her cheeks, and the blood
trickling down her naked back.   The indifference
with which every one of the company but myself
beheld all this, convinced me that it was the custom of the country

The dinner was, in the main, good enough.
That is to say, there was a plenty of things naturally good, but what was very remarkable, it was
brought up in wooden dishes, out of which they all
helped themselves with their fingers, knives and
forks not being in use in America, except among
a few English people.   There was a very suspicious dish on the table, which they called terrapin
soup, in which I observed what had exactly the
appearance of the fingers and toes of little negroes.
I afterwards learned that this was actually the case,
and that terrapin is the cant name for black chil-
dern, as papoose is for those of the Indians.   During the dessert, an unlucky slave happened to let
fall a knife to which he was helping his mistress,
who snatched it up in a great passion and gave
him a deep gash in the face.   I dropt my knife and
fork in astonishment, but nobody else seemed to
notice this horrible incident.

The next morning I strolled out into the fields
with a view of seeing the system of rural economy practised in the south. One of the best managed plantations, I was told, was that of his excellency Governor Hancock, whose name is signed
to the declaration of independence, said to be written by one Jefferson, a player belonging to the
Philadelphia theatre. The governor is a brisk,
troublesome little man, about forty. His plantation is at a place called Merrimack, on the river
of that name. I saw plenty of slaves, and a scarcity of every thing else. The principal products
are rice, cotton, and tobacco. The rice grows generally upon the high grounds; but the cotton
requires to be covered with water occasionally.
The best is called Sea Island, because it grows upon little islands in the mill ponds, which the people here, according to their universal practice of
hyperbole, call seas. As for the tobacco, this filthy
and unwholesome weed is found to flourish best in
the negro grave-yards, where it is commonly raised, and where you may every day during the
month of January, when it is ripe, see the children of the slaves gathering it from the very graves
of their parents. This tobacco is used as food by
men, women, and children, who eat it as we do
sallad. Here I saw the poor negroes working
bare-headed, and I might say bare backed, in the
broiling sun, which sometimes actually sets fire to
their woolly heads, of which I saw several examples in the course of my travels. Two or three

2*

heads were already beginning to smoke, and I was
told if I staid half an hour longer, I might see them
in a blaze. However, having seen enough to con-
vince me that the system of farming here was execrable, and finding it getting rather cold, I returned home by another route, which gave me an opportunity of seeing Yale college.

In reconnoitring about, I fell in with one of
the professors, to whom, willing to see whether
the poor man understood Latin, I paid my com-
pliments *in forma pauperis*. The professor, after
staring at me with a most ludicrous expression of
ignorant wonder, asked me whence I came, and
upon my answering "last from Charleston, South-
Carolina," shrugged up his shoulders and replied,
"it was really so far off, that he could not under-
take to direct me," although the steeples were full
in sight! From this we may judge of the state of
learning and information on this side the Pacific.
Being determined to hoax these poor souls, I filled
a box with pebbles, old mortar, and pieces of brick
bats, which I sent to the faculty as a valuable suite
of American minerals; whereupon they unani-
mously bestowed upon me the degree of doctor of
laws. There were some vitrified masses I picked
up near an old glass-house which caused great speculation, being considered unquestionable volcanic
productions. When questioned as to their locali-
ty, I sent them on a wild goose chase in search of
a burning mountain.

Becoming tired of Charleston, its negroes and tur-

key buzzards, (which the turbulent spirit of democracy has dubbed eagles,) and desirous of getting
to New-Orleans as early as possible, I took a seat
in the stage for Portsmouth, New-Hampshire, and
departed before daylight the next morning. When
it should have been daylight, the fog was so thick
it was impossible to see the leaders, and I expressed some apprehension. One of the passengers assured me, however, that as the driver was drunk,
as a matter of course, daylight was of no consequence—it was trusting to Providence at all events.
Indeed, I am assured by persons of veracity, that
travellers in this country place their chief dependence on the horses, who, being left pretty much
to themselves, in consequence of the intoxication
of the drivers, acquire a singular discretion, and
seldom run away except when the driver is sober.
Thus we travelled under the guidance of instinct,
till near ten o'clock, when objects gradually became visible along the road. The driver about
this time waked up, and I was congratulating myself on his appearing sober; but the same communicative passenger assured me it was of no consequence, for he would be drunk again by the time
breakfast was over.

I had heard a great deal about the populous-
ness of the country in the neighbourhood of Boston; but I can safely affirm, that during the whole
of this morning's ride, I saw neither house nor
human being along the road. We heard indeed a
deal of barking and howling at no great distance,

which the communicative passenger assured me
was that of various kinds of wild beasts, that abound
in these parts.   He told me they frequently surrounded the stage, devoured the horses, and if
their hunger was not then satisfied, topped off with
the driver and passengers.   Indeed, what with
mail robberies, which happened almost every night,
and attacks of wild beasts, there was little hope
of getting to the end of a journey of a dozen miles
alive.   " *Boutez en avant*," roared out a little
Frenchman in a corner, taking a great pinch of
snuff at the same time.   All this, thought I, comes
of the turbulent spirit of democracy.

Breakfasting at a little town, which, like all
other towns in this country, is called the city of
Hartford, I saw a young lady devour thirty-six
cucumbers, moistened with a quart of vinegar.
After which, she sat down, played Lodoiska on
the piano, and then went into the field to pull
onions. Such horrible incongruities are generated
in the rankness of democracy! There was a child
of about eight years old in the room, who called
for an antifogmatic, which he drank off at one
swallow, after which he lighted a cigar and amused himself with singeing the woolly pate of a little
black boy, or terrapin, as they call them when
made into soup. According to the prediction of
the communicative passenger, the driver was nodding again on his seat, in less than half an hour after
starting.   I was so provoked that I threatened to
lick him, as the naval officer said at Boston.   But

the communicative passenger cautioned me against this, assuring me the driver was a man of great consequence—a member of congress—judge of the court—colonel of militia—justice of the peace—deacon of the church—constable and keeper of the county jail withal. " So," continued the communicative passenger, " he can issue a warrant—take you in custody—try you for an assault—clap you in jail—keep watch over you when there—and finally have you prayed against by the whole congregation." " Diable !" exclaimed the little Frenchman in broken English ; " these democrat yankees have as many offices as their citizen hogs have hind legs." " Why, how many legs have our citizen hogs, as you call them, Monsieur ?" replied the communicative passenger. " Why, eight at least," said the other, " or they could never furnish the millions of hams which I see every where. Diable ! I have breakfasted upon ham—dined upon ham—and supped upon ham, every day since I arrived in this country. Yes, sir, it is certain your pigs must have at least eight hams a piece ;" upon which he politely offered me a pinch of snuff, which I refused with cold dignity. If I know myself, I have no national prejudices ; but I do hate Frenchmen.

Though anxious to gain information, I cannot condescend to mix with these rank republicans, ask questions, and take the usual means of gaining it. I wanted to know the reason of such a multiplicity of offices being united in one person ; but it was

enough for me to permit these low-lived scum of
democracy to give me information, without demeaning myself to ask for it.   Luckily the little
Frenchman, like all his detestable countrymen,
was fond of talking.   " Pray," said he, " how
comes it that his honour the colonel, deacon, stage-
driver, has so many offices ; or, as you yankees
say, so many irons in the fire? One would think
that men were as scarce in this country, as hams
are plenty."   " Why, the truth is," replied the
communicative traveller, " that being one of three
persons out of the whole county that can read, it
is necessary he should labour in a variety of voca-
tions, for the good of his country.   Besides, as
every democrat is by nature and habit a drunkard,
a sober man among them, is like a good singer at a
feast ; the one is knocked down for all the songs,
and the other is under the necessity of playing a
sort of jack-of-all-trades."   " Diable !" exclaimed
the little Frenchman, " do you call this colonel
stage-driver a sober man ?"   " Why not exactly,"
replied the other ; " but this valuable person has
been drinking so long, and so constantly, that habit has become second nature, and he is never so
wise, valiant, discreet, and pious, as when he is
full charged with apple brandy "   So much for
the spirit of democracy, thought I.

The country through which we passed, every
where exhibits traces of the lazy, ragged, and dirty
genius of democracy ; who prides himself on his
beggary, and riots in the want of all those ele-

gancies which civilized nations consider essential
to existence. A few miserable negro huts, without
roof or windows, and a few half-starved, half-naked
negroes, dot the sterile landscape here and there.
The only white people we saw, were a knot of
half-drunken savages, assembled about a log hut,
shooting at a mark. Here we stopped to water
the horses, and I looked about to see the mark at
which they were trying their skill. " You are
curious," said the communicative traveller, " to
know what they are shooting at. Look at that
little negro. They will tie him to yonder post
anon, and shoot at him till he is torn to atoms, as
they do at turkeys, for sixpence a shot." Another
proof of the horrible spirit of democracy. The
person who gave me this information added, that
when they had finished this trial of skill, they
would, in all probability, turn to and take a few
shots at each other for mere amusement.

We arrived at Portsmouth, an inland town,
capital of Georgia, where being heartily sick of
this bundling, guessing, tippling den of democracy,
I thought I would, for once, depart from my ordinary rule, and inquire when I might calculate on
getting to New-Orleans? I accordingly put the
question to the landlord ; but the little impatient
Frenchman who was close at my heels took the
word—" New-Orleans ! Diable ! are you going to
New-Orleans, Monsieur?" Thinking his surprise
might have some connexion with the yellow-fever,
I was thrown off my guard, and before I knew it,

condescended to answer—" Yes, I am," but with
cold dignity. The little villain took a huge pinch
of snuff, blew his nose like a trumpet, and exclaimed—" To New-Orleans! You are going to New-
Orleans, and I am going away from it as fast as I
possibly can! One of us must be going the wrong
way, that's certain. Pray," said he, turning to the
communicative traveller, " will Monsieur be good
enough to tell me whether I am travelling north or
south, to New-Orleans or Passamaquoddy?" " Due
north—in the very eye of the North star—to
Passamaquoddy, and not to New-Orleans, Monsieur," answered the other. " Monsieur," said
the little villain, turning to me, and offering a
pinch of snuff with a low bow—" Monsieur, when
you get into a stage coach, do you ever condescend
to inquire where it is going? I am an old traveller,
and as we are going to part, never perhaps to meet
again, let me conjure you, by the memory of your
ancestors and the victory of Waterloo, never to
set out on a journey without inquiring whither you
are going? However, Monsieur, it is an ill wind
that blows nobody good. I am going no farther
North than this place, shall finish my business
here this afternoon, and to-morrow, if Monsieur
pleases, we will set out for the South, which I assure
you is the very best way to New-Orleans." " And
I," said the communicative traveller, " shall also
return in the morning, and mean to go South as
far as the city of Charleston, so that we shall have
the pleasure of each other's company, for a thou-

sand miles at least." " A thousand miles!" replied I, for here again surprise overcame my dignified reserve—" Why, I thought"——. But I stopt short, being unwilling to give the little rascal of a Frenchman another laugh, by letting him into the secret of a certain blunder which shall be nameless. " On the whole," observed the communicative traveller, " you have not lost much by this little ride out of your way. You have had an opportunity of seeing one of the finest and best cultivated parts of the country ; and a portion of the most moral, as well as enlightened of the people. And you have lost no time by the little excursion, for I am credibly informed, such has been the mortality at New-Orleans, that there is not a single human being left alive there. Nay, the very dogs, cats, and parrots are extinct. You may as well wait, therefore, till it is peopled again, which will be very soon, for the folks in this country, particularly the democrats, don't mind dying in the summer, if they can only have a merry winter before hand." Here our conversation was interrupted by a loud cry of " Help—murder—help!" proceeding from an adjoining room. On running in to see what was the matter, we found a son of the landlord, (who by the way was a general,) about eight years of age, had thrown his mother down on the floor, and was beating, biting, scratching, and mauling her in a dreadful manner, while the general stood by laughing and clapping his hands in ecstacy, every moment crying out, " That's it

3

—that's my fine fellow—O! he'll make a brave republican!" Such are the first lessons of children in this chosen land of bundling, gouging, drunkenness, impertinence, impiety—and, to sum up all in one word, *democracy*.

Heaven be praised, thought I, the force of democracy can go no further; but I was mistaken with a vengeance. Just at this moment we had a terrible explosion, which I at first thought was the little Frenchman sneezing—but it turned out, on inquiry, to be something of a far different nature. Though my heart sickens at the bare recital, I shall give the story, for the benefit of all the admirers of democracy.

It seems a fellow of the name of Ramsbottom, a man-milliner by trade, and a roaring patriot, had taken offence at a neighbour, whose name was Higginbottom, because his wife had attempted to cheapen a crimped tucker, and afterwards reported that he sold his articles much dearer than his rival man-milliner over the way, whose name was Winterbottom, and whose next door neighbour, one Oddy, was Winterbottom's particular friend. In the pure spirit of democracy, Ramsbottom determined to dirk not only Higginbottom and his wife, and Winterbottom, and Oddy, and their wives; but all the young Higginbottoms, Winterbottoms, Oddys, and little Oddities. It was some years before Ramsbottom could get them all together, so as to make one job of it. At last he collected the whole party at his own house, to spend

their Christmas eve, and determined to execute his diabolical purpose. It appears, however,
from what followed, that he had previously changed his mind as to the dirking, probably because it
was too much trouble, (for these democrats hate
trouble above all things.) Just as they were up to
the eyes in a Christmas pye, the explosion took
place which I had just heard, and the whole party,
Ramsbottom, Higginbottom, Winterbottom, and
Oddy, together with their wives, and all the little
Ramsbottoms, Winterbottoms, Higginbottoms, Oddys and Oddities were all blown into such small
atoms, that not a vestige of them was to be found.
I saw their bodies afterwards, all terribly mangled
and torn to pieces. Such is the intense and never-
dying spirit of vengeance, generated by the turbulent spirit of democracy, that the desperado,
Ramsbottom, it appears, did not scruple, like the
republican Samson of old, to pull down destruction on himself, that he might be revenged on his
enemies.

CHAP. III.

Little Frenchman—Treatment of Slaves—Mode of baking saw-
dust cakes—Kitchen-furniture—Spirit of Democracy—Apostrophe—Mode of paying bills by the Yankees and French—
Little Frenchman again—Solitary inn—Attempt to rob and
murder the author—Bandit disguised as a stage-driver—Arrival at Boston—Gives the little Frenchman the slip.

IN order to get rid of the little Frenchman, with
his confounded mahogany face, gold ear-rings, and
dimity breeches, who seemed inclined to be im-
pertinently jocular with my mistaking the way to
New-Orleans, I determined to say nothing, but
defer my journey a day longer. Accordingly I
apprized the landlord of my intention, and suffered
the stage to depart without me. With a view to
keep up my dignity, as well as to acquire all the
information possible, in relation to the country,
its people, and manners, I determined to remain in
my room all day, take my meals in dignified re-
tirement, and seize every opportunity of questioning the waiter. From him I gathered many precious items, concerning the blessed effects of the
turbulent spirit of democracy.

He solemnly assured me, that all the servants
eat off the kitchen floor in these parts, which, instead of boards, is usually floored with mud, well
trodden by the pigs, which, in this land of equality, are admitted to all the privileges of citizenship,
vote at elections, and, I believe, are eligible to the
highest offices, provided they are natural born
pigs.   On my inquiry how they understood the
votes of these freeholders, he replied, that a grunt
was always considered as a suffrage in favour of
the democratic ticket, and a squeak for the federal
or aristocratic party.   Hence abundance of pains
is taken to teach the pigs either to grunt or squeal,
according as their owners belonged to one or other
party ; and many a vote was changed by certain
sly pinches of the pigs ears, as they were brought
up to give their suffrages.

The waiter further informed me, in the course
of my investigations into the kitchen, that the
poor servants, who are all blacks and slaves in this
part of the country, had neither beds nor covering
at night, but all pigged together in the same ashes,
where they often squabbled and fought all night,
either to get near a little live coal, or to keep each
other warm by exercise.   As to food, one may
guess, as these vulgar democrats say—one may
guess what that is, when I state, on the information of the waiter, that the week before I came to
Portsmouth, in this very kitchen, a murder was
committed by one gentleman of colour, on another,
in consequence of a dispute about the property of

3*

a bone, which had been picked six days in succes-
sion. The murderer at last seized the bone, hit
his adversary on the temple, and killed him instant-
ly : after which he buried him in the mud of the
kitchen, and sat himself quietly down to gnaw his
bone. The waiter further stated, that they were
allowed no cooking utensils, and that the way they
generally baked their bread, which is altogether of
saw-dust, was to lie down at night with their feet
to the fire, on the soles of which they placed the
cake. They then go to sleep, and by the time the
cake begins to burn their feet so as to wake them,
it is done. This saw-dust bread is their chief food ;
but candour obliges me to state, that once in a great
while they are treated to a bit of spoiled codfish,
or tainted pork, which makes them almost run
mad with ecstacy. Determined to make the most
of this meeting with such an intelligent fellow, I
continued to question him concerning the number
of pots, kettles, stew-pans, &c. in the kitchen—
their state, quality, and condition—whether they
had any knives and forks allowed them, and if the
latter had three prongs? Whether the little negroes
were taught their prayers ; and whether the pigs
were permitted to eat out of the same dish with
them ? Touching the pots and kettles, he assured
me, upon his honour, that there was but one pot,
with one ear, in the whole establishment ; that the
kettle was still worse off than the pot, having had
no handle within the memory of man ; that the
only knife they had was half a stump of a blade,

without edge or point, which, however, was rather a lucky circumstance, since, as they were always fighting at meals on account of the scarcity prevailing, they would do mischief if they had knives; that, as to forks, it was the landlady's maxim that fingers were made before knives and forks ; that the little people of colour were taught nothing but swearing, and that the pigs always breakfasted before them, on account of being considered freeholders, and entitled to vote.

In this way I gained more insight into the nature of the turbulent spirit of democracy, than if I had mixed with half the people of the town, and asked as many questions as a yankee democrat. Indeed I had read in all our books of travels, that these bundling, gouging republicans, although they asked a dozen questions in a minute, were principled against answering any. This I was told by the waiter, arose, in a great degree, from almost every white man being generally in court a dozen or twenty times a year, for some offence or other, (principally that of murder,) by which means they got a habit of being shy in answering interrogatories. " But," said I, at the conclusion of my examination, " how does it happen that you are so plump and well clad, if your fellows are thus naked and starved?" ", Why," replied the fellow, showing his white teeth from ear to ear— " Why, if master must know, I make a point of helping myself out of the dishes, as I go in and out ; and my master keeps me well dressed, for the ho-

nour of the house." Alas! thought I to myself,
here is another proof of the demoralizing effects of
slavery! This honest man is obliged to descend to
the degradation of rifling apple tarts, and embez-
zling mouthfuls of mutton, to keep himself from
starving!—O, Wilberforce! well mayest thou en-
danger the lives of all the white people of the West
Indies, in thy attempts to benefit the blacks!—O,
Buxton! well mayest thou be permitted to poison
half the people of London with thine execrable
small beer, in consideration of thy godlike philanthropy!—And, O, Betty *Martin!* well mayest
thou be allowed to hunt, shoot, and hang up the
wild Irish, in consideration of thine eloquent
speeches in parliament, in behalf of brawned pigs,
crammed turkies, and plugged lobsters!

In the evening I paid my bill, which seemed
rather to astonish the landlord, and in truth it was
a most swingeing one. At first I demurred—but
upon the poor fellow assuring me he was obliged
to charge strangers, particularly Englishmen, tre-
ble, and sometimes quadruple, to make up for the
losses sustained by his own countrymen, and the
Frenchmen, who generally went away without
paying at all, I paid him with the air of an English nobleman, expecting he would dub me My
Lord; but he received the money with perfect indifference, and did not even condescend to bow or
thank me. Such is the influence of the turbulent
spirit of democracy!

In the morning, as usual in all parts of this

country, we set forth before daylight, so that I could not see my fellow-passengers. Two reasons combine to produce this republican custom of travelling before day, and after dark. In the first place, it gives opportunity for robbing the stages, the drivers and owners of which, as I am assured, are, generally, in league with the bands of robbers which infest all parts of this country, to the number, sometimes, of two or three thousand in a band. In the second place, as there is generally one or two pick-pockets in every stage-coach, and forty or fifty in every steam-boat, the darkness gives a capital scope for the exercise of this fashionable republican vocation. Aware of this, I always rode with my hands in my pockets, and was now indulging in this salutary precaution, when a sudden jolt of the jarvie brought my head in full contact with the back of a passenger on the seat before me. " Diable!" exclaimed a voice which seemed to be familiar to me, and then all was silent again. Not long after, there exploded a sneeze which shook the whole vehicle. " My G—d !" ejaculated I, " I'm sure I've heard that sneeze before ; it must be my little Frenchman!"—But there was no help for it now, and I determined to keep him at an awful distance.

Daylight showed the mahogany face, gold earrings, and dimity breeches of the little Frenchman, and by his side the communicative traveller. All at once it occurred to my mind, that these two men were accomplices in some scheme for robbing me. What confirmed me in the suspicion was, the confounded civilities of the little Frenchman, who expressed infinite pleasure on the occasion, and offered me a pinch of snuff every two minutes. "We thought we had lost you," said he "and were regretting the absence of such an agreeable companion." I made no reply but by a stiff inclination of the head, and continued with my hands in my pockets, my pocket-book in one, and my watch in the other. "Pray, Monsieur, what a clock is it?" said the Frenchman. Aha! thought I, are you thereabouts? So I told him my watch had run down, and held it faster than ever.

This mode of disposing of my hands was very inconvenient on these rough democratic roads. and occasioned me to bounce about, to the no small annoyance of these Jonathans, who threw out divers unmannerly hints, which I treated with perfect contempt. "He must have his pockets full of guineas," said the little Frenchman in a whisper, winking at the same time at the communicative traveller. I understood all this perfectly, and when we stopt to dine, managed to exhibit a neat pair of hair triggers to these two worthies, who exchanged very significant looks thereupon. "It won't do," observed one to the other, in a desponding tone.

The house we put up at for the night was in a lonely wood, at a distance of several miles from any human habitation. The owls whooped, the

wolves howled, the whippoorwills whistled, the
frogs croaked, the caty-dids, caty-didded it, the
crickets chirped, and every sound seemed fraught
with melancholy thoughts and mournful anticipa-
tions.   During supper, and afterwards, I perceived an exchange of mysterious looks between the
Frenchman, his companion, the landlord, and his
wife, and detected them in various secret confer-
ences.   In one of these I overheard the landlady
say, in reply to some question of the communicative traveller, who seemed to be an old acquaintance, " we killed him last night, poor old creature ;
I was almost sorry for him."   My blood ran cold
—some poor old traveller, doubtless, thought I.

Having very little doubt but there was a plan to
rob and murder me in this lonely place, I determined to defeat it by sitting up all night with a
pistol cocked in each hand, ready to defend myself.   In spite of the hints and questions, and en-
treaties of the landlord and his wife, I persevered
in my plan, although I was obliged to take to the
kitchen fire, under pretence that they were going
to make up a bed for themselves in the room where
I was.   In this situation I continued, a pistol ready cocked in each hand, until, as I judge, about
two or three o'clock, when a door suddenly opened and a bandit cautiously entered with a dark lantern in his hand.   Thinking there was no time to
be lost, I let fly at him, and he fell flat on his face
bellowing murder with all his might.   Immediately there was a great stir ; the landlord, his wife,
children, servants, the stage passengers, and lastly

the little Frenchman and the communicative traveller bounced in, helter skelter, crying out "what's
the matter—what's the matter." I stood with the
other pistol ready to fire, and bade them approach
at their peril. "Diable!" exclaimed the little
Frenchman, stooping down to examine the body,
" he has killed our driver." " Not exactly,"
cried the fellow, jumping on his two legs as brisk
as a grasshopper—" but if I don't have him up
before the justice for shooting at a fellow for only
coming in to light his, lantern, to see to put together his horses, darn my soul." I insisted upon it,
he was a genuine bandit, and that he had come into the kitchen on purpose to rob and murder, or at
least keep me in custody till my friends paid my
ransom. But I found they were all in league
against me, and was finally glad to compound with
the pretended stage-driver, by treating him to a
pint of whiskey. It is thus that strangers are always served in this democratic paradise. They
must either sit still and be murdered by inches, or
pay a composition for defending themselves. To
carry on the deception, the fellow with a dark lantern was actually mounted on the coach box, with
a view, I suppose, of making a more successful attempt the next night. But in this he was disappointed, for the moment we got to Boston, I took
my portmanteau under my arm, darted round a
corner, and hid myself in a remote part of the city.
In my retreat I heard the little Frenchman ex-
claim, "Diable ! this is what you call taking
French leave, I think."

CHAP. IV.

The author congratulates himself on having got rid of the little
Frenchman—Is in danger of being twice robbed and murdered
—Neglect of common decency in taverns and steam-boats—
No knives and forks—Dirty hands and faces—Astonishing
number of people with one eye, or two black eyes—Expla-
nation of Governor Hancock—Gouging—Spirit of Democracy
—Leaves Boston—Passes through Ohio, Alabama, and Connecticut—Attempt to rob the mail on Sunday by a foot-pad, who
turns out to be a deacon of the church—Amusements of the
people—Holy alliance—Bellows Falls—Steam-boats invented
by Dr. Isaac Watts, who wrote the Book of Psalms—Ignorance
of the Yankees of the points of the compass—Their mode of
navigation—Little Frenchman again—Mode of deciding elections—Rudeness of boatmen and captain—Attempt of the little
Frenchman to rob the author.

"THANK heaven," said I, " I've got rid of the
little Frenchman, the bandit, and his whole crew,"
as I seated myself snugly in the quiet retreat of a
hotel in a remote part of the city. I slept pretty
soundly that night, with the exception of two attempts to rob and murder me, one by a person who
opened my door, but who seeing the barking iron,
shrunk back and pretended to have mistaken the

room; the other by the chamber-maid, who came
in after I had gone to bed with an excuse that she
had forgot to put water in my pitcher. By the
way nothing can equal the neglect of these turbulent democrats in all the common decencies of life,
particularly washing their hands and faces. On
board the steam-boats, where there are perhaps a
hundred people, one does not see above two or
three washing themselves of a morning. As they
use no knives and forks, either for want of knowing their uses, or for fear the passengers would
steal them, it is easy to conceive the disgust an
Englishman must feel at seeing them diving in the
dishes with their filthy fingers. Another characteristic feature of these people is, that more than
one half of them want an eye, and those that happen to have two, generally exhibit a black ring
round one or both. On inquiring into the cause
of this peculiarity, I was told by his excellency,
Governor Hancock, that men, women, and children, were so given to fighting and gouging, that
it was next to a miracle to see one of them without the want of an eye, or at least a pair of black
eyes, which is reckoned a great beauty in these
parts. So much for the turbulent spirit of democracy, thought I to myself

Having staid three days to give the little Frenchman, the bandit, and the rest of them a fair start,
I thought I might safely proceed on to the south;
accordingly I took passage in a stage and departed
the fourth morning, as usual before day-light, for

the convenience of being robbed and murdered on
the way. This happens generally about three
times a week; but it is in the true spirit of democracy to sport with property and life. Our road
carried us through the states of Ohio, Alabama,
and Connecticut, among the people of steady
habits, as they are denominated. All I can say is,
that the sooner they change these steady habits the
better, for it will hardly be believed, that we had
scarcely entered the confines of Connecticut, the
very centre of steady habits, when, although it
was Sunday, (a sufficient reason for deterring any
christian highwaymen,) we were stopt by a foot-
pad, who demanded money with as little com-
punction as a he-wolf. Upon my showing my
pistols, however, he sheered off, and the driver
whipping up his horses at the moment, we luckily escaped this time. The incident of a single
foot-pad attempting thus to rob a whole stage load
of people, furnishes another proof of the fact, that
stage-drivers and stage-owners, not to say a majority of stage-passengers, are accomplices of these
bands of robbers. Had it not been for my pistols,
we should all have been robbed to a certainty, and
most probably the rest of the passengers would
have shared my spoils. What exhibits the turbulent and impious spirit of democracy in all its
turpitude, is the fact that the driver, after getting
fairly out of sight, turned round to the passengers
with a grin, and exclaimed, " I guess I've distanced the deacon." So that this foot-pad was one of
the pillars of the church !

I have nothing to add in addition to these disgusting details, except that as far as my sight could reach on either side of the road, I could see nobody at work but the poor gentlemen of colour, half clothed, as usual. The white people were for the most part employed in getting drunk at the taverns, running horses, fighting cocks, or gouging one another's eyes out—the women sitting along the road, chewing tobacco, and spitting in the faces of passers by; and the little boys and girls were pretty much engaged in beating their parents. To vary these amusements, they sometimes made a party to hunt a little naked negro with their dogs, which I observed were all blood-hounds. My heart bled to see these cruel mastiffs, less cruel indeed than the turbulent spirit of democracy, tugging at their naked haunches, and I could not help invoking the philanthropic genius of the holy alliance to interfere in behalf of these oppressed beings.

About five in the afternoon we arrived at Bellows Falls, at the mouth of the Ohio, where I embarked in the steam-boat for New-York. These steam-boats, all the world knows, were invented by Isaac Watts, who wrote the book of psalms. Yet the spirit of democracy, as usual, has claimed the honour for one Moulton, or Fulton, I forget which; although it is a notorious fact, that Isaac Watts died before this Fulton was born. This settles the question. But there is no stopping the mouth of a genuine democrat. Our course lay

upon a river which the Yankees call the East river, although, to my certain knowledge, it runs directly west. But it would be tasking the ignorant
spirit of democracy too much to suppose its vota-
ries could possibly tell the points of the compass.
Indeed I was credibly informed, that their most ex-
perienced navigators universally judge of their
course within soundings by the colour of the mud
or sand, which adheres to the lead, and when this
fails them, trust to Providence.

While sitting in a state of indolent and contemptuous abstraction, with my back to as many of the
company as possible, I was roused by a sneeze,
that I could have sworn to in any part of the
world. "It is the c——d little Frenchman! Here's
Monsieur Tonson come again!" I would as soon
have heard the last trumpet as this infernal explosion. In a few minutes he espied me, and coming
up with the most provoking expression of old ac-
quaintanceship, offered me a pinch of snuff—"Ah!
Monsieur, I am so happy! Diable!—my friend
and I thought we had lost our agreeable companion;" and, thereupon, he made me a delectable
low French bow, that brought his long nose within an inch of the deck—he then left me for a moment, and returned with his friend the veritable
communicative traveller, who had the insolence
to claim acquaintance, from having travelled a few
days in the same stage with me. A good sample
of the forward, impudent spirit of democracy! I
expected every moment to see the great bandit with

*4

his dark lantern, to complete the trio, but for
some reason or other he didn't make his appearance.   " Ah! Monsieur," cried the little Frenchman, " you don't know how we have missed your
agreeable society.   Diable! we have not had a
good laugh since we parted."   Then he offered
me a pinch of snuff, a civility which he repeated
at least a hundred times, in the course of the day,
though I always declined it in the most dignified
and contemptuous manner.

Disgusted with every thing I saw, and most especially with this rencontre, I determined to mortify these free and easy gentry, by taking not the
least notice of any person whatever, and going
without my dinner, on purpose to spite them.   Many of the women looked hard at me, with an
evident desire to be taken notice of; but I always
turned my head away, resolved to have nothing to
say to them.   Several persons also came round,
and made attempts to engage me in conversation,
but I answered them in monosyllables, and they
went away, whistling to hide their mortification.
My contempt for the little Frenchman increased
every moment, by observing the pains he took to
be agreeable.   He talked, laughed, bowed, offered
his box to every one that came in his way, and
complimented the women, till all were delighted
with him, and he seemed as much at home as if he
had been born and brought up among them.   Des-
picable subserviency! contemptible hypocrisy! to

pretend to be pleased with these scum of democracy.

When the dinner-bell rang I remained on deck,
until one of the waiters came up to tell me dinner
was ready I took no notice of him. In a few
minutes the little Frenchman assailed me. " Is
Monsieur ill ?" " No!" said I. " No? Eh bien—
what is the matter? Ah ! I guess, as these Yankees
say. If Monsieur has no money, never mind, I
will pay for his dinner." Come, come, I replied
in great wrath, at his infernal mistake, upon
which he went down, and as I afterwards learned,
proposed a subscription for a poor passenger, who
was obliged to go without his dinner, for want of
money to pay for it. One may judge of the humanity of these people, from the fact that not one
of them contributed a cent. One woman turned
up her nose, and exclaimed, " Marry come up—
I thought as much ; pride and poverty generally go
together." Another declared she would not give
a pin, to save such a rude humgruffian from starving ; and a third pronounced me a strolling player
out of employ. The communicative traveller, on
coming up after dinner, endeavoured to comfort
me for the loss of my meal, by observing I had not
missed much by it. " There is nothing but snatching and quarrelling for the favourite bits, and the
ladies did nothing but scold, and pull caps. Then
it is, just as likely as not, you would have been
seated between two greasy engine men in red flan-

nel shirts, one a negro perhaps, (for they all dine together,) who would have made no scruple of gouging one of your eyes out, if you had happened to get possession of one of their tit-bits. You were well out of the scrape." Glorious spirit of democracy, thought I to myself.

Towards evening the boat stopped at a place called the city of Annapolis. Every thing is a city here. A blacksmith's shop, with a church, and a pig-sty, is a city, and must have its corporation, if it be only that the spirit of democracy may revel in a little brief authority. An office of any kind is their darling, and a whole state will be convulsed about the election of a constable. These elections are generally carried in the last resort by the cudgel and gouging; and I am assured that the number of one-eyed people, and people with black rings round their eyes, is generally doubled by one of these struggles of principle. As we approached the wharf, I was standing among a coil of ropes, with my back towards the great city, when one of these sticklers for equality, in a red flannel shirt, came up and desired me to move out of the way. The fellow was civil enough, for that matter, but I only answered his impertinent intrusion with a look of withering contempt. — Upon this, he gathered a part of the rope in coils, in his right hand, and when we were ten or a dozen yards from the wharf, threw it with all his force, with a design to knock a person down, who stood there. But the chap was too dexterous for him, and caught the end of the rope in his hands, which he immediately fastened to a post. The whole brunt of this Yankee joke fell upon me, for my feet being entangled in the end of the rope thus thrown, it tripped up my heels and laid me sprawling on the deck. The little Frenchman officiously helped me up, and offered me a pinch of snuff, by way of comfort; but as for the democratic gentry, they seemed rather to enjoy the thing, and if the truth was known, I dare say were at the bottom of the joke. I cursed the fellow heartily; but he coolly answered—" 'Twas your own fault; I asked you to get out of the way." So much for the turbulent spirit of democracy.

I stept ashore, to escape the giggling of these polite republicans, and rambled to the distance of a couple of hundred yards. While here, I heard a bell toll, and then a hallooing, and saw them making signals for me to come on board; but I was determined to treat them all with silent contempt, and continued my walk in a direction the other way. The shouting continued, and I don't know how far I might have strolled, if I had not been suddenly roused by the noise of the boat's wheels. Turning round, I found the vessel was fairly under way; whereupon I condescended to run and halloo as hard as I could bawl. After some little delay the wheels were stopped, and a boat sent off to take me on board, where, instead of making an apology, the brute of a captain told me I deserved to have been left behind. " If it had not been for the persuasions of your friend," pointing to the little Frenchman, " you might have staid ashore till next trip, and welcome." " *My* friend," exclaimed I, turning to the officious little mahogany man with a look of withering contempt, which he returned by offering his box, and assuring me he would not have lost my charming society for the world. These persevering civilities on his part, and especially this last impertinent interference, confirmed me in my suspicions, that there was a deep-laid plan to rob and murder me the first convenient opportunity. What added weight to these apprehensions, was the fact of my continually detecting him and his companion, the communicative traveller, conferring together every now and then, with divers shrugs on the part of the Frenchman, and significant smiles on that of his friend.

When we came to draw lots for our births, it was so managed by the captain, (who was no doubt an accomplice,) that I drew a birth in a remote part of the vessel, forward. But, owing to some failure in the plot, the little Frenchman and his companion, both drew births in the after cabin, which I perceived disconcerted them not a little. But they soon rectified the mistake ; for upon the complaints of two feeble old gentlemen, that they should find it fatiguing to go into the forward cabin, the Frenchman seized the pretext, and with

one of his confounded low bows, offered his birth
to one of the cripples, while his companion did
the same to the other. I saw through all this, and
determined to play them a trick, by lying awake
all night, to watch them, with my pistols ready.

Late in the night, and when all the lights were
out, I heard somebody get out of a birth on the
opposite side where the little Frenchman slept.—
The person went upon deck, and after staying a
minute or two, groped his way down again, and
cautiously approached where I lay, with my pistol cocked. Presently he laid his hand upon my
throat, doubtless with an intent to choak me first,
and rob me afterwards, at leisure. At this instant
I fired my pistol, just as the little Frenchman ejaculated, in a whisper, " Diable ! I am lost !" Confusion reigned, lights were brought, and the whole
affair was disclosed. I solemnly charged the little Frenchman, who had escaped my shot, with
an attempt to rob and murder me ; while he as solemnly asseverated, that he had got up upon a necessary occasion, and, on his return, took the right
hand instead of the left, by which means he had
encountered my birth instead of his own, which
was directly opposite. The passengers, captain
and all, being, without doubt, accomplices in this
attempt, sided with the Frenchman ; believed
every word he said, and gravely advised me to
take care how I fired pistols in the cabin of a steam-
boat. This was all the satisfaction I got for this
nefarious attempt. The little Frenchman even

had the assurance to play the injured party, and actually offered to forget and forgive. " It was all a mistake," said he, " and let us think no more of it." So he offered me a pinch of snuff, which I rejected with dignified contempt.

CHAP. V.

Frogs-Neck—Bull-Frogs—Hell-Gate—Impious spirit of democracy—Mode of passing Hell-Gate— Fondness of the Yankees
for dying accounted for—Dutch courage—Mr. Robert James—
Country seats—Sandy-Hook—Navy-Yard, &c.—Little Frenchman—Author takes lodgings with a gentleman of colour at the
Hotel des Huitres—Bill of exchange—Unprincipled behaviour of
the Yankee merchant—Quarterly Review—Description of New-
York—Basis of republicanism—Agrarian Law—Quarterly—
Classification of the citizens of New-York—Extensive circulation of the Quarterly Review—Gratitude of the people of colour—Beggarly pride of republicanism—Propensity to thieving
among the higher classes—Picture of the manners and morals
of the people, drawn by the landlord—Quantity of flies and
moschetoes—Law against killing spiders—Little Frenchman,
&c.

ABOUT daylight I was roused by a most horrible
noise, which resembled nothing I had ever heard
before. On going upon deck, I perceived the
whole surface of the water, as far as the eye could
reach, covered with immense bull-frogs, who leapt
and croaked, to the infinite delight of these taste-
ful democrats, who were all gathered together to
hear this charming concert, which they would pre-

fer to the commemoration of Handel Some of the
largest of these frogs actually jumped upon deck,
and a canoe alongside was nearly upset by three or
four of them clambering up its sides, at one and
the same time. The place is called *Frog's Neck,*
and never was there a spot more aptly named.
There is a little settlement near this, called New-
Rochelle, peopled by Frenchmen, who were doubtless attracted by the frogs. But such is the ardour
of these refined republicans, for this species of music, that the legislature has enacted a law, making
it death to kill one of these delightful musicians.
To kill a man here is a trifle—but to kill a frog is
capital!

Shortly after leaving Frog's Neck, we came to
the famous pass of Hell Gate, as it is impiously
called by the profane spirit of democracy. It is
the *Scilly* and *Charybdis* of the new world, and
nothing but the special protection of Providence
can account for the few deliverances that happen
to these reckless republicans in passing it, which
they do every hour of the day and night. As soon
as they begin to distinguish its roaring, which can
be heard at a distance of thirty miles, except when
the frog concert intervenes, all hands, captain, pi-
lot, and the rest, set to and drink apple brandy,
or whiskey, so that by the time they come to the
Hog's Back, they are as drunk as swine. They
then lie down flat on their faces and let the vessel
take her course. This preparatory tippling is
what they impiously call receiving " extreme

unction," and preparing for death, which the communicative traveller assured me not more than one out of three escaped on an average. I could not help expressing my wonder, that these people should thus recklessly sport with their lives. "O, as to that," replied he, " what with the curse of democracy, the grinding oppressions of unrestrained liberty, together with the total insecurity of property under mob law ; and the total insecurity of person, in consequence of the universal practice of robbery and murder, of which you have had ample experience,—I say, what with all this, ninety-nine in a hundred of these, my wretched countrymen, would as soon die as not, and some of them a great deal rather, only to escape the blessings of democracy." " But," said I, " why don't these miserable creatures say their prayers, and make some little preparation to die like christians, instead of thus beastifying themselves?" " O," answered he, with a coolness that made me shudder, " this is what we call *Dutch courage;* and I assure you, upon my credit, that I never knew a genuine brother Jonathan who could be brought to face an enemy, or die with decency, unless he had his SKIN full of whiskey, and was well ' *corned,*' as we say. This was the way in which we gained all our victories last war both by sea and land." Good, thought I, here is the testimony of one of their own countrymen. Mr. James shall add this to his apologies for Blue and Buff, in his next edition.

This conversation happened after safely passing this tremendous strait, which we did as it were by miracle. Betwixt this and New-York, the communicative traveller pointed out to me some two or three of what he called magnificent country seats, which seemed to me about the size of a pigeonhouse. I took no notice of him or them, but affected to be in a fit of abstraction, with my eyes fixed on vacancy. Turning the point of Sandy-Hook, we came in full sight of the city, its bay, and islands. I saw that several of these people were watching to detect in me some symptoms of surprise or admiration, so I resolved to disappoint them, and turned my back to the city, keeping my eyes fixed on the opposite shore. The communicative traveller, supposing I was looking at the Navy-Yard, where several large ships were lying, observed: "That is the Cyane, near the red store. Or perhaps you mean the other—that is the Macedonian—or perhaps you mean the one next her—that is ——." I could stand it no longer, but was fain to turn round and look at their detestable city.

When we came near the wharf, the little Frenchman came up to me with a low bow and the offer of his box as usual. "I hope Monsieur, my friend and myself shall take lodgings together. As we are strangers in a strange place, 'tis pity we should part. I assure you I shall not rob Monsieur," said he, with an impertinent, significant smile. I told him at last I should lodge that night on

board, and depart the next day in the same boat
I came. "What!" replied he, "is Monsieur
going to New-Orleans again? But in truth we
are sorry to lose your very agreeable company,
Monsieur, and hope we shall meet again when you
come back from New-Orleans." So saying, he
bowed profoundly low and departed, accompanied by his friend, and by my most devout wishes
never to set eyes upon either of them again.

Desirous to avoid any public attentions, and
most especially to escape the honour of being made
a citizen of New-York, which the corporation insist upon bestowing upon every stranger of distinction, in order to add some little respectability to
their sty of democracy, I took a private lodging
with a respectable man of colour who kept the Hotel des Huitres in Water-street. According to the
fashionable London mode, I intended to direct all
those who asked my address, to the City Hotel,
where there is generally such a concourse of people
that the bar-keeper never knows the names of half
the boarders. My first business after taking possession of my lodgings, was to present a bill of exchange, drawn on one of the most respectable merchants here, (if such a term can be applied to a
Yankee peddler,) by one of our first London bank-
ers.

I found him in his counting-room with a jug,
as I presume of whiskey, at his side, and pretty
well "corned," as the communicative traveller
says, though it was hardly nine o'clock. He received me with a sort of bear-like republican civi-

5*

lity, which I ascribed to the awe in which they stand of Englishmen, to whom they are one and all indebted more than they ever mean to pay. He read my letter, looked very deliberately at the bill of exchange, then folding them both up carefully, offered them to me. "Is it convenient for you," said I, "to cash the bill at once?" "No sir, not very convenient." "I suppose, then, I must be content with your acceptance at the usual sight." "My good friend, I don't mean to accept it, I assure you." "No, sir?" said I, bristling up, for I began to suspect some Yankee trick—"and pray may I take the liberty of asking the reason of this extraordinary conduct?" "Certainly. The banker who drew this bill, by my last advices is a bankrupt and a swindler. He has no effects in my hands, nor is he ever likely to have. I am sorry for your disappointment, but I cannot accept your bill of exchange." I snatched the letter out of his hand and hurried out of the room, and my disappointment was almost balanced by the pleasure I felt at this early confirmation of my impressions with regard to the character of these republican merchants, who I was satisfied, from reading the Quarterly Review, never paid a debt of any kind, there being no law in this country to oblige them. I had no doubt but the story of the drawer of my bill, (no less a man than Mr. Henry Fauntleroy, who keeps two mistresses, and three splendid establishments,) being a bankrupt and swindler, was a fabrication, invented to evade the payment. Such is the universal practice here, and thus is the reputation of half the merchants of Britain ruined in this country. The genuine republican merchant never stops payment and compounds with his creditors, (which they generally do twice or thrice a year,) without putting it all upon his correspondents in England, who are, in fact, always the greatest sufferers. This story they all make a point of believing, because they are all, or soon expect to be, in the same predicament. It is a proof of the generous credulity of honest John Bull that he still continues to trust, and be cheated by the turbulent spirit of democracy, as the editors of the Quarterly Review justly style it, in their usual strain of genteel irony.

Relating the story of my disappointment to my worthy landlord, I thought he looked rather shy, as if he expected it to be the prelude to a long score. But I at once satisfied his doubts by showing him a few guineas, and telling him I always paid my bill every Saturday night. He then resumed his confidence, and proceeded to let me into the secrets of this unprincipled and profligate city, which being the general rendezvous of people from all parts of this puissant and polished republic, (as the Quarterly calls it,) presents at one view a picture of the blessings of pure and undefiled democracy. That my readers may have the clearer idea of a genuine republican city, I shall be more particular in my description, especially as this is considered as the very pink of all the cities of the new world.

New-York, the capital of the state of New-Jersey, so called from being originally settled by Yorkshire horse jockies, is situated on the main land, between two rivers, about the size of the Thames, though not quite so large, that being unquestionably the greatest river in the world. That on the east they call the north, and that on the west, the east river, by a very pardonable blunder, as it would be taxing the spirit of democracy too severely to preserve the least acquaintance with such aristocratic trumpery as the points of the compass. The blessings of ignorance, constitute the basis of republicanism, as the Quarterly says, with its characteristic wit and humour.

Most of the houses are built of pine boards, and generally about half finished, the owners for the most part stopping payment before the work is completed. There is a great appearance of bustle, but very little business in fact, as the spirit of democracy impels these people to make a great noise about nothing. To see one of their peddling merchants staring about in Wall-street, one would suppose he was overwhelmed with the most momentous affairs, when, if the truth was known, his whole morning's business consists in purchasing a dozen birch brooms, or a pound of wafers. There is also a great appearance of building here, but this is partly owing to the necessity of new houses to replace the old ones, which generally tumble to

pieces at the end of three or four years, and partly
owing to the inveterate habit of emigration characteristic of the restless spirit of democracy, which
prevents the people remaining long in one place.
Hence they are perpetually on the move from one
part of the city to another. Sometimes whole
streets are deserted in this way, and then as new
buildings become necessary, the cry of these republican braggarts, as the Quarterly calls them, is
about the number of houses building, and the vast
increase of the city. Sometimes they pull down
a street and build it up again, merely to impose
upon strangers an idea of its prosperity, and attract
emigrants from England, although those who have
been weak enough to come hither for the last six
or eight years, are, with the exception of a few
sent home by the British Consul, every soul of
them on the parish.

The people of New-York may be divided into
three classes, those that beg, those that borrow,
and those that steal. Not unfrequently, however,
all these professions are united in one person, as
they are a very ingenious people, and almost every
man is a sort of Jack of all trades. The beggars
constitute about one third of the population, and
are supported with great liberality by the other
two classes, who remembering that charity covers
a multitude of sins, make use of its broad mantle
in this way, and upon the strength of their alms,
claim the privilege of borrowing without ever in-
tending to pay, and robbing Peter to give away to

Paul.   One of the most popular preachers here, is a most notorious gambler, but, at the same time, is considered little less than a saint, because he professes to give all his winnings to the poor. Another person, an alderman, generally breaks into a neighbour's house every night, but as he gives away all his plunder in alms, he is one of the most popular men in the city.   Another, who is a judge of the court, generally manages to pick the pockets of both the parties in a suit, and the jury think themselves lucky to escape ; yet he is adored for his liberality, and the beggars who all vote like the pigs, talk of running him for the next governor.

The borrowers consist of the most fashionable portion of the community, the people who give parties, ride in their coaches, and hold their heads considerably higher than the beggars.   The most approved mode of practising this thriving business is this : A gentleman gives a grand entertainment to a select number of friends, each of whom he manages to intercept as they go out, and make them pay pretty handsomely for dinner in the shape of a loan.   When one set gets tired, he invites another, and so on till his debts amount to sufficient to make it worth while, when he affects to stop payment, as he calls it, though he never began yet; takes the benefit of the laws for encouraging debt and extravagance, and on the score of his numerous charities, is generally recommended for some public office.   This is the last resort of

rogues, in this pure republican system, as the
Quarterly affirms. My landlord, the gentleman of
colour, who was in the habit of waiting at many
of these great dinners, assured me he did not recollect but a single instance in which the guests
escaped paying the piper in this way, when the en-
tertainer let them off, in consequence of having
picked their pockets at table. I asked him how
it happened that the guests did not resent or complain of this treatment. " O," replied he, " it is
diamond cut diamond—every one has his turn,
and it amounts to an equal division of property in
the end—a republican Agrarian law, as the Quarterly says." " What, do you read the Quarterly?"
said I. " O yes; we all read Massa Quarterly—
he love us people of colour so much." He further
assured me the people of colour had it one time in
contemplation to send out half a dozen of their
prettiest ebony lasses to England, that the gentlemen of the Quarterly might have their choice of
them for wives. But the ladies of colour, having
been persuaded by some of the white belles of fashion, who envied their high destinies, that all these
gentlemen lived in *Grub-street*, one of the most
ungenteel places in all London, turned up their
pretty pug noses, and demurred to the proposition.

I was delighted at this information, which not
only proved the extensive circulation of this valuable Review, but likewise the gratitude of the people of colour for the exertions of its conductors in
their behalf. It is enough to make the eye of phi-

lanthropy water to hear as I have done that such
is the pride of these beggarly republicans, that
they will not admit a gentleman or lady of colour
to any intimacy of association, insomuch that it is
considered a disgrace to enter into a matrimonial
connexion with them !   This is another beautiful
illustration of the beggarly pride of these upstart
republicans, as the Quarterly says.

The class of pick-pockets, shop-lifters, and
thieves of all sorts, is probably the most numerous of the whole community.   Nobody ventures
to carry money in his pocket, and when the ladies go out shopping, they always hold their
purses in their hands.   Even this is no security, for it generally happens that they are snatched
away before they have gone a hundred yards.
One of the shop-keepers here assured me it seldom
happened that a lady came into his shop without
pocketing a piece of lace, a pair of gloves, or something of the kind, provided they could not get at
the till.   It is the universal practice to search them
before they depart; and from long habit they submit to this as quietly as lambs.   Plenty of company to keep them in countenance, and long habit
renders them indifferent to discovery, as the shopman assured me.   Two or three ladies came in
meanwhile, and were suffered to go away without
being searched by the shopman, who, as I found
to my cost afterwards, was all this while busily
employed in emptying my pockets.   Yet, for all
this, do these bragging republicans boast that it is

unnecessary for the country people to lock their doors at night. My landlord assured me that this was the fact, but that it arose from the conviction that locking them would be of no service, every man being exceedingly expert in picking locks, both from education and habit.

"The consequence of all this," continued the worthy gentleman of colour, "is a general, I may say irremediable relaxation of manners, and a total want of prudence and principle in all classes. Drunkenness, impiety, insolence, extravagance, ignorance, brutality, gluttony, and every vice that can disgrace human nature, are the ordinary characteristics of these spawn of filthy democracy, as the Quarterly says; and if there be any thing in which these people are not utterly detestable, it is their fondness for oysters, which enables me to get a tolerable livelihood. This fondness is sharpened by the exquisite relish of breaking the laws at the same time that they gratify their appetites—the corporation of the city, for the purpose of monopolizing, having enacted that no oysters shall be brought to market, but what they eat themselves." Nothing, indeed, can equal the tyranny of the laws in this country; nor would it be possible to live under them, did not the turbulent spirit of demo- cracy compound for itself, by breaking them all without ceremony.

It is another consequence of the relaxation of morals among these virtuous republicans, that the relaxation of the laws, is in proportion to the re-

laxation of morals. To such an extent has this
been carried, that these people may be said to have
no laws at all. All sorts of crimes are here committed with perfect impunity; and it is a common
saying, that it requires more interest to be hanged,
than to attain to the highest dignity of the republic. Drunkenness is here the usual and infallible
apology for crime; and as the mass of the people
are usually *corned*, as my friend the communicative traveller says, this excuse is seldom out of
place. But what puzzled me, after seeing all this,
was, that the jails, bridewells, and penitentiaries,
which abound in almost every street, were full of
people. My worthy landlord, however, explain-
ed this to my satisfaction, by assuring me that such
was the abject poverty and consequent misery of
a large portion of these patent republicans, (as the
Quarterly says,) that they actually broke into these
receptacles by force, being certain of getting board
and lodging for nothing.

I was struck with the quantity of flies and moschetoes that infest the streets and houses all the
year round, and fly into one's nose and ears at every cor-enient opportunity, where the latter sing
most melodiously. To remedy this intolerable
grievance, there is luckily a species of spider,
which spins its web across the opening of the ear,
in which these insects are caught. It is no uncommon thing to see half a dozen or more flies and
moschetoes dangling in the ear of a fine lady.
There is a law to prevent the destruction of these

spiders, as there is against killing the turkey-buz-
zards, which abound here, and are the only street
scavengers, if we except the citizen pig freeholders, as the Quarterly calls them.

64

CHAP. VI.

NEW-YORK.

Total absence of religion—Indivisibility of a king and a divinity
and of democracy and impiety—Examples of the Puritans and
Charles the Second—Necessity of wealth, honours, and exclusive privileges, to the very existence of religion—Quarterly—
Barbarous love of finery—Mode of procuring it—Ignorance—
Story of a bluestocking—Lord Bacon—Ill manners—Total neglect of education—American chancellor of the exchequer can't
write his name—House of representatives obliged to have a
clerk to read for them!—Attempt of an English lady to establish a boarding school, and its result—French dancing-mas-
ters, how treated, &c.

ONE of the first things that disgusts a pious man,
as all Englishmen, particularly English travellers,
are, is the horrible profanation of the Sabbath in
this town. This contempt of religion and its ob-
servances arises partly out of the turbulent spirit of
democracy, and partly from the want of a privileged church establishment, such as has made Great-
Britain the bulwark of religion in all ages. There
is in the first place such a natural and indivisible
association between a king reigning over his peo-

pel by divine right, and divinity itself, that it is next to impossible a true subject should not be a true believer. On the contrary, the pure spirit of democracy, which rejects the divine right of kings, will naturally resist every other divine right, and thus it has happened that impiety and rebellion have ever gone hand in hand. Every person versed in the history of England must be familiar with innumerable examples of this truth. Waving a reference to all others, it is sufficient to recollect the total relaxation of religion and morals which prevailed among the Puritans who rebelled against Charles the martyr, and the brilliant revival of piety and the church on the accession of his son. In fact, it is a maxim with all orthodox writers, that a pious people will always be obedient to their sovereign, not so much because he governs well, as because he governs by divine right.

A few obvious positions will in like manner demonstrate the absolute necessity of a liberally endowed, exclusively privileged church establishment, like that of England. Money is universally held to be the sinew of war; and inasmuch as money is essentially necessary to enable the sovereign to defend and maintain the rights and interests of the government, so is it equally necessary to enable the bishops and dignitaries of the church to defend the consciences of the people against the dissenters, and all other enemies of the church. It is a pure democratic absurdity to suppose that men,

6*

will fight for their country from mere patriotic
feelings, or that they will preach for nothing.
Hence it is essentially necessary, that both should
be equally well paid; for as the promise of the
plunder of a city stimulates the soldier to acts
of heroism, so in like manner will the promise of
a good living of ten or fifteen thousand sterling a
year, equally stimulate the dignitary of the established church to fight the good fight of faith the
more manfully.

In fact, as the Quarterly says, "the want of
an established church has made the bulk of the people either infidels or fanatics." There will never be any pure religion here until they have an
archbishop of Armagh with 60,000 acres of glebe,
and a bishop of Derry with 150,000. It is these
and similar noble establishments in Ireland that
have made the people of that country so orthodox,
and so devoted to the king.

This mode of stimulating the zeal of pious dignitaries by wealth and honours, is accompanied with
other special advantages. In proportion as the
hierarchy is enriched by the spoils of the people,
the latter becoming comparatively poor, are pre-
cluded by necessity from indulging in vicious extravagance and corrupt enjoyments. They will
practise per force, abstinence, economy, self denial, and the other domestic virtues so essential
to the welfare of the lower orders. Hence it is
sufficiently obvious that in proportion as you cur-
tail the superfluities of the commonalty by taxes,

tithes, high rents, and poor rates, you guaranty to them the practice of almost all the cardinal virtues. Again: In proportion as the people become poor, they will necessarily pay less attention to the education of their children; and I fear no denial, except from radicals, democrats, and atheists, when I assert, that considering the mischievous books now in circulation on the subject of liberty and such impieties, the greatest blessing that could possibly happen to the lower orders would be the loss of the dangerous faculty of reading. In no age of the world were this class of people so devoted to the honour of the priests, and the glory of their kings, and consequently to the interests of religion and human rights, as when a large portion of them could not read, and were without any property they could call their own. I appeal to the whole history of mankind for proof of the maxim, that ignorance and poverty are the two pillars of a privileged church, and the divine right of kings.

It may be urged by radicals, democrats, and unbelievers, that the same rule which ordains the diminution of certain vices by the absence, equally ordains their proportionate increase by the multiplication of the means of their gratification. That consequently the rich prelates and nobility must necessarily become corrupt in proportion to the increase of their wealth. But even admitting this to be true, the people are gainers by the arrangement, since, by this means, their sins and transgressions are shifted upon their superiors, who an-

swer the end of a sort of scape-goats, or peace of-
ferings, under cover of which the poor entirely
escape. It is therefore plain, that the more rich
and wicked the privileged few become, the more
will the lower orders be exempt from both. Let
us hear no more then of the impious slang of democracy, as the Quarterly says, which would persuade poor deluded innocence and ignorance that
equal rights and a general diffusion of knowledge,
answer any other end than to make people thieves,
murderers, gougers, bundlers, unbelievers, blasphemers, rowdies, and regulators, and, to sum up
all in one word, republicans.

When it is recollected, therefore, that the essence of the turbulent spirit of democracy consists
equally in the rejection of the divine right of the
king, and the equally divine right of the bishops,
and deans, and arch-deacons, to their thousands a
year, it will readily be conceded that a pure republican cannot possibly have any religion. Accordingly, as I before observed, the first thing that
strikes a stranger who is used to the exemplary
modes of keeping the Sabbath in London and all
other parts of England, is the total neglect of that
day in all parts of the United States. In New-
York, indeed, there are plenty of churches, but
they were all built before the millennium of democracy, as the Quarterly says, and under the pious
auspices of our established church. The first thing
these blessed republicans did when they returned
to the city, on the conclusion of the peace, was to

break all the church windows, and so they have remained ever since. One of them has a ring of eight copper kettles, instead of bells, which being rung by the old deaf sexton, gives singular satisfaction to the commonalty—I beg pardon—the sovereign people—who assemble on Sundays to dance to the music in front of the church. As to going to church to hear divine service, nobody pretends to such anti-republican foolery. The shops are all kept open on Sundays, so that one can see no difference between that and any other day, except that the good folks drink twice as much whiskey, and put on their Sunday suits, in which they stagger about with infinite dignity, until finally they generally tumble into the gutter, spoil their finery, and sleep themselves sober. Such are the genuine habits of the turbulent spirit of democracy, as the Quarterly says. My worthy landlord assured me that the African church was the only one in which there was a chance of hearing a sermon, and that even there, the whole congregation was sometimes taken up and carried to the watch-house, under pretence that they disturbed the neighbourhood with their groanings, howlings, and other demonstrations of genuine piety. The true reason was, however, that these bundling, gouging democrats, as the Quarterly calls them, have such a bitter hostility to all sorts of religion, that they cannot bear even the poor negroes should sing psalms. However, as it is the first duty of a christian to hide the faults, and draw a veil over the transgres-

sions of his fellow-men, I shall abstain from any
further comments on the horrible depravity of republicanism in general, and Yankee republicanism
in particular.   I must not omit to mention, however, that in this, as well as every other town in
the United States, there is a society for the propa-
gation of unbelief, secretly supported by the government, most of the principal officers of which
are members.   Their exertions were inveterate
and unceasing, and they displayed the same zeal
in making an atheist of a devout christian that we
do in the conversion of a Jew.   Of late these societies have remitted their labours in consequence
of there being no more christians to work upon.

The love of dress, glitter, and finery, is one of
the characteristics of a rude and republican people;
of course we see it displayed here in all its barbarous extravagance.   Every thing they can beg,
borrow, hire, or steal, is put on their backs, and a
fine lady somewhat resembles a vessel dressed in
the colours of all nations.   It is impossible to tell
what flag she sails under.   This finery is for the
most part hired by the day of the milliners and
pawn-brokers, and there are dresses which can be
had at from two shillings to a dollar a day.   The
first young ladies of the city, who never know
their own minds, but alway " guess" at it, as the
Quarterly says, principally figure in these hired
dresses; and it is by no means uncommon for one
of them to be hauled out of the city assembly or a
fashionable party by a pawn-broker, in consequence

of having kept the dress longer than the time specified.   One might suppose such an accident would
disturb the harmony of the company, but the other
young ladies continue to dance away without taking any notice of the unfortunate Cinderella, thus
stript of her finery, or perhaps content themselves
with *guessing* what the matter may be.   I ought
to mention here, that though the young ladies always " guess," the young gentlemen are commonly given to " reckoning" upon a thing, a phrase
which becomes exceedingly familiar by a long habit of running up scores at taverns.

Notwithstanding all the cant and boasting of
these turbulent democrats about the necessity of
education to self-government, the general diffusion
of intelligence, and all that sort of thing, it is most
amazing to see the ignorance of the best educated
people here.   A young lady of the first fashion,
who can read writing, is considered a phenomenon: while she who has read Lord Byron is held
a blue stocking, and avoided by all the dandies for
fear she should puzzle them with her learning.
Such, indeed, is the natural antipathy of genuine
republicanism to all sorts of literature, that the only possible way of teaching the little children their
a, b, c, is by appealing to their inordinate appetites in the shape of gingerbread letters well sweet-
ened with molasses.   The seduction is irresistible,
for no genuine Yankee republican can make head
against treacle.   I one night, at a literary party,
happened to mention some opinion from Lord Ba-

con to a young lady who had the reputation of being rather *blue*. " Bacon—Bacon," replied she
briskly—" O! I *guess* we call it gammon. But
we don't put ' *Lord*' to it, because it's anti-republican." I took occasion to apprize her with as little appearance of contempt as possible, that *our*
Bacon was not gammon, nor ham, but no less a
personage than the present Lord Chancellor of
England, the sole inventor and propounder of human reason, and the noble art of philosophy. " I
guess he must have made a power of money by
it," said the learned lady. " Did he get a *patten*
for his invention. We always get *pattens* for any
great discoveries in *Amerrykey*." Upon this she
started up, ran giggling over to some of her *set*,
and continued the whole evening laughing at me,
thus joining ill manners to ignorance. But what
can you expect from a gang of barbarians, among
whom learning is considered anti-republican, as the
young lady said ; where, to be able to read, is an
insuperable obstacle to promotion, and where the
present Chancellor of the Exchequer of the United States, who is considered as one of their best
scholars, signs his name with a *fac-simile*, that is,
by deputy ? This deputy they were obliged to
send to England for, on account of the few persons
who could write being all engaged in forging the
signatures of bank notes. Even the house of representatives, where all the wisdom and learning of
the nation assembles, is obliged to employ a clerk
to read the papers, messages, &c., for the edifica-

tion of the country members, whose education has been neglected in that respect.

To sum up my remarks on the subject of literature here, I may say with perfect truth and impartiality, that the education of youth consists in learning to drink whiskey, eat tobacco, love dirt and debauchery, despise religion, and hate kings. An English lady attempted to establish a boarding-school for young ladies a few years ago, but the genius of democracy would not submit to her salutary restrictions. The young ladies first pouted, then broke into the kitchen, where they devoured all they could find, and came very near eating up the black cook, and finally set fire to the house, and ran away by the light of it; since then, nobody has been hardy enough to set up a school for young ladies, except two or three desperate Frenchmen. These confine themselves to teaching them to dance, which being an art congenial to savages, they acquire with considerable docility. They sometimes, to be sure, pummel the poor Frenchmen black and blue with the heels of their shoes; but candour obliges me to say, that I never heard of their tearing the dancing master in pieces, or eating him up alive.

7

CHAP. VII.

NEW-YORK.

Quotations from the Quarterly—Poverty of invention and want of originality of republicans—Dr. Watts—Emigrants, their situation here—Story of one—Author advises him to go home and tell his story to the editor of the Quarterly—Promises him a free passage to England—Reflections, &c.

ONE may truly say, with the Quarterly,* "the scum of all the earth is drifted into New-York,' notwithstanding what Miss Wright and Captain Hall may affirm to the contrary, in their flippant farragoes and "prostitute rhapsodies, and of impiety, malevolence, and radical trash," as the Quarterly says. " Godless reprobates, brutal and ferocious tyrants, thieves, swindlers, and murderers," as the Quarterly says, " make up the mass of the population." " Robberies, burglaries, and attempts at murder, disgrace the city every day ; and one cannot walk the streets in the daylight. without seeing fellows lay in the gutters, with broken legs, arms, &c. who continue, day after day, without being noticed by the nightly watch, or the open day of humanity, to roast in the sun, and

---

* Vide No. 58, Eng. Ed.

be devoured by the flies," as the Quarterly says.
Indeed, I can safely, and from experience, affirm
the Quarterly is perfectly justified in asserting
that, " Insolence of demeanour is mistaken for
high-minded independence." No reputable English
traveller ever saw man, woman, or child, blush
here, except a few English people, not yet pro-
perly acclimated—that the speeches of lawyers and
members of congress are all jargon and nonsense—
that the preachers of the gospel all bellow out their
sermons in their shirt sleeves—that the judges are,
for the most part, worse criminals than those they
try—that dogs are trained to hunt young negroes,
instead of to point game—that men, women,
children, negroes, strangers, all congregate together at night, in one room—that not one in ten
of the slaves die a natural death, being, for the
most part, whipped till they mortify, and the flies
eat them—that the moral air is putrid—that the
land is all hung up in the air to dry—that the air
is one animated region of flies, moschetoes, and
other noxious insects; and that such is the influence
of the turbulent spirit of democracy, not only upon
the moral and physical qualities of the people, but
upon the very elements themselves, that the one
is not less perverted than the other. All this I
am ready to swear to, and so is the Quarterly Review. Respect for the precept of our pure English orthodoxy, which inculcates charity and good
will to all men, prevents my indulging any further
upon this topic. For the present, I will content

myself with summing up the characters of these
patent republicans, in the words of the Quarterly.

" Fools must not come here, for the Americans
are naturally cold, jealous, suspicious, and knavish
—without any sense of honour. They believe
every man a rogue until they see the contrary—
and there is no other way of managing them except by bullying. They have nothing original ;
all that is good or new is done by foreigners, and
yet they boast eternally."* In proof of this I may
add, that they claim every thing, and have even
attempted, as I before observed, to rob poor Dr.
Watts of the credit of having invented the steam-
boat. I have little doubt but they will lay claim
to his psalm book before long. There is every day
some invention trumped up here, which has been
exploded and forgotten in England, and for which
a patent is procured without any difficulty. It is
only to swear to its originality, and that is a ceremony, which no genuine republican will hesitate
a moment in going through. This city is full of
foreigners ; but what can possibly induce them to
come here, I cannot conceive. I have not met
with a single Englishman that was not grumbling
at his situation, and discontented with every thing
around him. The inns are filthy—the boarding
houses not fit to live in—the waiters negligent and
saucy—the wines poison—and the cooking execrable. Yet they remain here with an unwarrantable pertinacity, in spite not only of the Quarterly,

* Vide No. 58, Eng. Ed.

out of the bitter lessons of experience they receive
every hour.

One morning as I was walking up Chestnut-street,
the principal promenade in New-York, I saw a
poor drunken fellow wallowing in the gutter, and
talking to himself about Old England. This circumstance, together with his dialect, which partook
somewhat of the Yorkshire purity, excited my
curiosity and commiseration. I helped him up,
conducted him to my lodgings, and put him to bed
to sleep himself sober. After waking, and refresh-
ing himself with a dozen stewed oysters, I inquired
his history. His tale so happily illustrates the common fate of English emigrants, to this El Dorado,
(as the Quarterly calls it,) that I shall give it in
his own words, as nearly as possible. The poor
man could neither read or write, and had been, as
will be perceived, the dupe of those interested
speculators and agents of this government, who
write books to deceive the ignorant and unwary
English.

"I was very comfortably situated in Old England, the land of liberty, religion, and roast beef,
except that one-fourth of my earnings went to the
tax-gatherer, another to the poor rates, and another to the parson and landlord. But still, as I
said before, I was happy and contented; when I
happened to read Mr. Birkbeck's "radical trash,"
as the Quarterly says, which turned my head,
and put me quite out of conceit with the blessings of English roast beef and English liberty.
*7

Just about this time, the man came round, to tax my house, my land, my horses, oxen, cattle, servants, windows, and a dozen or two more small matters. A little while after the parson sent for his tithes, the landlord for his rent, and the overseers of the poor for the poor rates. All these coming just upon the back of Mr. Birkbeck's mischievous book, put me quite out of patience, so I made up my mind to emigrate to America.

" I sold off all that I had, turned it into English guineas, and went down to Liverpool, where I took passage. Supposing I should have no use for money in the States, after paying my passage, I spent the rest in treating my fellow passengers at the tavern, and set sail with empty pockets, yet full of spirits. The Captain was a full-blooded Yankee democrat, and the greatest little tyrant in the world. He held that it was much better to steal than to labour,* and by way of illustrating his theory, robbed me of twenty guineas on the passage. On my remonstrating with him, he told me that it was the universal custom of his country, and I might make it up on my arrival in New-York, by robbing the first man I met with.

" Our passage was long, and as the Captain had not laid in half provisions enough, we were obliged to cast lots, at the end of a fortnight, who should be killed and eaten. The first lot fell upon me, but I bribed a poor simple fellow with a

* Vide 58th No. of the Quarterly

guinea, to take my place. Our Captain insisted
upon the privilege of knocking the man on the
head, it being one of his greatest delights; there
was nothing he preferred to it, except hunting little people of colour with bloodhounds. Out of ten
passengers in the steerage, I was the only one that
got to New-York alive, the rest being all killed
and eaten. When I stepped ashore, I was so hungry, and had got such an inveterate habit of eating
human flesh, that I immediately laid hold of a fat
fellow, and bit a piece out of his cheek. Unluckily he turned out to be an alderman, and I was
forthwith taken to the Bridewell, where I made
acquaintance with several of the most fashionable
people of the city, who generally spend a part of
their time there. I had read of this in the Quarterly, but did not believe it till now; and when I
get home to Old England, I intend to publish it all
in a book of travels. I shall make a good round
sum by it, if I can only get one of the Reviewers
to write it down for me, and say a good word in
the way of criticism.

" The Bridewell is a pleasant place enough. Once
a week they have an assembly; on Sunday they
play at all fours, and every day in the week they
tipple delightfully, in company with the judges of
the court, the corporation, and a select number of
the clergy. For my part, I should not have minded spending the rest of my days there; but this
was too great a luxury. So I was turned out at
the end of a fortnight, to make room for a lady of

fashion, who was caught stealing a pig in Broad-
way. From the Bridewell I went sauntering
down the street, expecting every moment some
one would call out to me to come and do some little job, and pay me a dollar for it. But I might
have saved myself the trouble for not a soul took the
least notice of me, until at last an honest fellow
slapped me on the shoulder, called me country-
man, and asked me into a tavern to take a swipes.

"Having been somewhat corrupted by the fashionable society in Bridewell, I suffered myself to
be seduced, and went in with him. Here, while
we sat drinking, I told him my situation, and the
difficulty I had in getting employment. He asked
me if I was a sober man, and on my assuring him
I never drank any thing stronger than water, exclaimed, 'By my soul, brother, but that is the
very reason. Nobody ever thinks of employing
a sober man here, and if you look for work till
doomsday, you will never find it, unless you qualify yourself by seeing double, by which means
you'll get two jobs for one.' I told him I had no
money, and if I had, nothing should tempt me to
drink. 'O, ho!' cried he, 'You've no money
to pay your shot, have you?' So he fell upon me,
and gouged out both my eyes, besides biting off a
good part of my nose, under pretence that I had
spunged upon him, as he called it; but the landlord
afterwards assured me, it was only because I would
not drink, it being the custom here to beat people

JOHN BULL IN AMERICA.

to death, or roast them alive, if they won't get drunk.

"Finding it was the custom of the country, and that there was no getting along without it, and that drink I must or starve, I took to the bottle, and soon got employment, in sweeping the streets and other miscellaneous matters. Agreeably to the good old maxims of English prudence, I determined, in my own mind, only to drink up three-fourths of my wages, and save the rest, to buy a farm in the western country, where I intended to go and set up for a member of congress, when I had qualified myself by being able to walk a crack after swallowing half a gallon of whiskey. But my prudential resolves were of no avail, for the gentlemen sweepers told me it was against the law to save our wages. On my demurring to this, they took me before the judge, who decreed me a beating, besides taking away the money I had saved, which he laid out in liquor, and we got merry together.

"Seeing there was no use in laying up money, I thought it best to follow the custom, and from that time, regularly spent at night what I earned during the day. I led a jolly life of it, but it was, like the Bridewell, too good to last for ever. I fell sick owing to the unhealthiness of the climate, where a large portion of the people die off every year.— They carried me to the hospital, where they would not give me a mouthful of liquor; kept me upon soup diet, and cut off my leg by way of experi-

ment, with a handsaw. How I ever got well, and
got my leg on again, I can not tell ; but you
will hardly believe it, when I assure you, that after
keeping me here in perfect idleness for six weeks.
and curing me, they most inhumanly turned me
out into the streets to begin the world again! That
emigrants to this land of promise. should be obliged
to work for a living, was too bad, and I determined not to submit to such an imposition ; so I snapt
my fingers at them, swore I would see them hanged first, and threatened them with the vengeance
of the Quarterly. ' This is a pretty free country, to
be sure,' said I, ' where a poor emigrant is obliged to work for a living.'

"Walking in a melancholy mood down the street,
I all at once thought of what the captain of the
Yankee ship told me about its being the universal
opinion and practice here, that it was much easier
to get a thing by stealing than working for it.
This sophistry of the captain corrupted me on the
spot, and I took the first opportunity of putting
the theory into practice by cabbaging a watch out
of a window, which hung so invitingly that I could
not resist the temptation. I put it into my pocket till I got to the church, where I pulled it out in
order to set it by the clock. Just at that moment
a fellow with all the characteristic insolence of
democracy, (as the Quarterly says,) laid hold of
me and the watch, and before I could muster pre
sence of mind to knock the impudent rascal down,
carried me to the police, where I was examined

and committed. Instead of enjoying myself in jail for a year or two, according to the custom of old England, before trial, I was brought up the very next day, tried, sentenced, and accommodated for three years in the State Prison, before I could say Jack Robinson. It was in vain I pleaded the custom of the country, appealed to the sacred name of liberty, and to the authority of the Yankee captain. The judge coolly told me that the custom of the country only applied to native born citizens, and that not being even naturalized, I deserved more exemplary punishment for trespassing upon the peculiar privileges of the free-born sons of liberty. 'By the time you get out of prison,' said his honour, ' you will be qualified for citizenship, and may then steal as many watches as you please.' I bowed, thanked his lordship, who, by the way, neither wore gown nor wig—only think! and withdrew to go through my initiation into citizenship.

" People may talk of the State Prison, but for my part, if any thing could tempt me longer to breathe the pure air of liberty in this land of hog-stealing judges,* and shoe-making magistrates, it would be the hope of spending three more such happy years. I had plenty of meat every day, (which to a hard-working man of the land of roast beef was enchanting, if only on account of its novelty,) did not work half so hard as at home, and

* Vide 58 No.

as for the loss of liberty, to any person who reads
the Quarterly, that must be considered a great
blessing.   They were obliged to turn me out neck
and heels, at the end of my delightful seclusion.
In revenge I picked the turnkey's pocket, got glo-
riously fuddled, and was ruminating in delightful
recollections of old England, when your lordship
found, and carried me home with you.   By the
way, I should like a few more of those capital oysters.   To make an end, I am now balancing whether
I shall take out my citizenship, and thus qualify
myself for the Yankee mode of sporting; steal
another watch before I become privileged, and so
get into that paradise, the State Prison again; or
apply for a free passage to the land of liberty and
roast beef.   They tell me I shall be provided for
if I will give a certificate that it is impossible for
an English emigrant to exist in this country.   For
my part, I am not particular, and am ready to say,
or swear to any thing, to be revenged on these
bloody Yankees, who first put a man in jail, and
then turn him out again, against all the rules of
liberty and good government."

I advised the poor man to go home to England,
and promised to get him a free passage.   I also
gave him a letter to the editor of the Quarterly,
requesting him to take down his story, and make
an article of it in his next number, for the purpose of deterring all his deluded countrymen from
adventuring to this land of bundling gouging,
guessing, and democracy.   The fate of this poor

deluded, honest, and industrious emigrant, ought
to be a warning to all those who sigh for the
blessings of pure democracy, and believe in the
impious, radical slang of Miss Wright, Captain
Hall, Birkbeck, and the rest of the polluted, putrid, pestilent, radical fry, as the Quarterly says.
The best of these English emigrants are actually
obliged to work for a living, and if they are not
lucky enough to get into the Bridewell or State
Prison, more than two-thirds of them actually starve
to death.

S

CHAP. VIII.

THE more I see of the people of this country,
the more I am struck with the seeming inconsis-
tencies that I every day encounter. That they
are the greatest cowards in existence is clear, from
the repeated assertions of the Quarterly—yet they
are continually fighting and quarrelling. That
they are utterly destitute of every feeling of personal honour,* is proved by the same authority ;
and yet the young men are all duelists, and risk
their lives every day upon the point of honour.
There is no country in the world, as I have before stated, where thieving, house-breaking, and
murder are so common, and yet the shop-keep

* Vide No. 58, Eng. Ed.

ers hang out their richest goods at the doors
and windows; the housewives leave their clothes
out all night to bleach or dry; the country people
leave their implements in the fields without scruple, and there is a general carelessness in this respect, which would seem to indicate an honest and
virtuous people.   But a little study and attention,
soon lets one into the secret of all this, and the ex-
planation becomes perfectly easy.

That quarrelsome people, and those who run
wantonly into danger, are, for the most part, cowards, is demonstrable.   He, for instance, that seeks
to quarrel, seeks to fight—he that seeks to fight,
seeks to die—he that seeks to die, seeks never to
fight more—and he that seeks never to fight more,
is a coward.   To explain the seeming contradic-
tion to the old maxim, that knavery is always suspicious of others, it is only necessary to refer to
the fact, that people careless of their own property, are generally the most apt to make free with
that of others, and this constitutes the very essence
of the spirit of democracy.   The people don't
mind being robbed, because they can easily reim-
burse themselves by plundering their neighbours of
twice the amount.   Indeed such is the inveterate
passion for pilfering, that it is no uncommon thing
for a man to rob himself, that he may have an excuse for making reprisals upon his friends.   On
one occasion I went into a jeweller's shop, which I
found deserted by every body.   After staying
long enough to have filled my pockets with jew-

els, the shopman came in, and glancing his eyes round to see if all was safe, seemed very much mortified that I had not robbed him. I heard him mutter to himself, " one of your d——d honest Englishmen."

It is in this manner that the society of which the pure spirit of democracy forms the basis is consti-tuted; and this is what is practically meant by equal rights. It puzzled me at first, how a socie-ty so constituted, could possibly subsist for any length of time. But the wonder is easily explain-ed. To be free, a people must be in a state of barbarity—to be in a state of barbarity, is to ap-proach to a state of nature—to approach to a state of nature, is to come near it—to come very near it, is to be on the verge—and to be on the verge, is ten to one to fall in. Hence a free people must be in a state of nature, where we know all things are in common, and consequently all men thieves. If it be urged, that a people in a state of nature can have no system of laws, I answer that there is no essential difference between a people who have no laws, and a people who pay no regard to them. The pure spirit of democracy is nothing but a state of nature, as the Quarterly has sufficiently prov ed; and the people of this country are all bund ling, gouging, scalping, guessing, spitting, swear-ing, unbelieving democrats.*

In my various walks about the city I visited the

*Vide No. 58. Eng. Ed.

Park, as it is called, and the Battery, the pride and boast of these modest republicans. The Park is situated at the intersection of Hudson and Duane-streets, and is very nearly, or quite, large enough for bleaching a pair of sheets and a pillowcase all at once. Judging from newspaper puffs, you would suppose it was an elegant promenade, encompass-ed with iron railing; but I may hope to be believ-ed when I assure my readers that no one walks there but pigs and washerwomen, and that the part of the fence which still remains, is nothing but pine. There is no other Park in the city.—But the Battery! O, you should see the Battery—for seeing is believing. I visited it on Sunday after-noon, when I was told I should see it in all its glo-ry. I saw what we should call a wharf jutting out into a sluggish puddle, about half a quarter of a mile wide, which they call a bay. On this wharf were a few poles stuck up—they had no leaves or limbs, but I was assured they would grow in time. The place stunk intolerably, but whether owing to the stagnant pool, called, in the republican verna-cular the bay, or to the filthy nastiness of the peo-ple walking there, I cannot say. Here I saw hun-dreds, not to say thousands of people, strutting, or rather staggering, about in dirty finery. Some hug-ging and kissing each other with the most nause-ating gusto of lust, heated by whiskey—others singing indecent and impious songs—but the ma-jority of them, in the true spirit of democracy, gouging and dirking each other for amusement.

8*

In one corner might be seen a group wallowing
and rolling about in the mud like drunken swine
—in another, half a dozen poor wretches gouged
or dirked, writhing in agony amid the shouts
of the people—and in a third, a heap of mis
erable victims in the last stage of yellow fever.
Nobody discovered the least sympathy for them,
and here no doubt they perished with a burning
fever, exposed to a broiling sun, with the thermometer at 110 degrees, the usual temperature of this
climate, winter and summer.   Here they remained to have their eyes stung out by moschetoes
while living, and to be devoured by flies when
dead.   I shuddered at the scene, and turned to
another quarter in hopes of seeing a boxing match.
or some polite, refined exhibition, but in vain.
Such is the celebrated promenade of the Battery
at New-York; such the Sunday amusements of
enlightened and virtuous democracy!   Nothing
could equal the gross and vulgar impiety of their
conversation, of which the following specimens
will furnish examples:

No. 1.—" Well, neighbour, how d'ye get on?"
        " O, by degrees, *as lawyers go to
        heaven!*"
No. 2.—" When do you go out of town?"
        " Why, I think of going to-morrow,
        God willing."
No. 3.—" *Bless my soul,* neighbour, where
        have you sprung from?"

" *Why, God love you,* I sprung from
the clouds, *like Methusaleh !*"

No. 4.—" Well, friend, how does the good woman to-day ?"

" Why thank you, *she complains of
being a little better !*"

Enough of this. One's blood runs cold at such
impious profanity. Indeed, the people are, one
and all, grossly indelicate and impious in conversation, as the Quarterly says.*

To vary the scene, and to obliterate in some degree the painful impressions occasioned by the
groups I have attempted to describe, I strolled into
the play-house, which is always open on Sundays,
from ten in the morning till any time the next
morning. But I only got out of the frying pan
into the fire, for such a bear-garden never christian
man unluckily entered. The theatre is nothing
more than a barn, abandoned by the owner, as not
worth being rebuilt, with a thatched roof, and stalls
for a good number of cattle, which are now con-
verted into boxes for the *beau monde.* The hay-
mow is now the gallery, and the rest is all boxes.
Shakspeare being considered anti-republican, and
the English dramatists generally unpopular, the
exhibition consisted of a drama, the production of
a first-rate republican genius. The plot cannot be
unravelled by mortal man; but the catastrophe
consisted in the heroine of the piece being drank

---

* Vide Quarterly, No. 58, Eng. Ed.

for by some three or four admirers. It is to be understood that there is no sham here. All is real drinking; the audience will endure nothing less, and the pleasure consists in the actors all getting really and substantially drunk.   This is what the best republican critics call copying life and manners, of which the aggregate here consists in drunkenness, impiety, and debauchery.* The successful hero, who carried off the lady, swallowed three quarts of whiskey, the only liquor considered classical, and such was the delight of the audience, that one and all cried out, " Encore! encore! let him drink three more!" The hero, however, hiccupped an apology, hoping the audience would excuse the repetition. He is considered the Roscius of the age, and thought far superior to Kean, or Cooke, though the latter was rather a favourite, on account of his once having paid court to the national taste, by performing the character of Cato, elegantly drunk.   This they called the true conception of the part, it being utterly impossible to admit the idea of a sober patriot or republican. The notion savours of aristocracy, and one would run the risk of being tarred and feathered, by suggesting such a heterodoxy in politics.

It is one of the most unanswerable proofs of that total want of genius, invention, and originality, with which these people have been justly charged, that the plays represented at this theatre, and throughout the whole of the United States, are entirely of British manufacture.   Were it not for

* Vide Quarterly, No. 58, Eng. Ed.

Shakspeare, Milton, Newton, Locke, Bacon, Professor Porson, and a few more illustrious English dramatic writers, the theatres in this country could not exist.   Shakspeare's Tom and Jerry is played over and over again, night after night ; and Bacon's Abridgement as often, if not oftener.   Another proof is, that they import all their actors from England, it being a singular fact, that although the people are actually drunk two-thirds of the time, such is their poverty of intellect, that they cannot play the character of a tippler with any remote resemblance to nature.   They seem, indeed, destined to put all old maxims to the route, and among the rest that of " Practice makes perfect;" since none are so frequently intoxicated, and yet none play the character with so little discrimination.

While indulging in comparisons connected with the superiority of Englishmen, English horses, dogs, beer, beef, statesmen, various reviewers, travellers, poets, pick-pockets, philanthropists, tipplers, and tragedians, over all people, and more especially this wretched scum of democracy,* I was roused by a sneeze, which went to my very heart.   A horrid presentiment came over me; I dared not look in that direction, but remained torpid and inanimate, till I saw an open snuff-box reached over from behind, and slowly approach my nose.   'Twas the little Frenchman, with his mahogany face, gold ear-rings, and dimity breeches !

---

* Vide Quarterly, No. 58, Eng. Ed.

" Ah ! monsieur—monsieur—is it you? I am so happy ! Are you going to New-Orleans yet? I hope monsieur has not been robbed and murdered above once or twice, since I had the pleasure to part from his agreeable company?" I received him, as usual, with a look of freezing contempt; but this had no effect upon the creature, who continued to chatter away and bore me with his confounded snuff, till I was out of all patience. I should, most certainly, have tweaked his nose, had I not been previously warned by the communicative traveller, that he was a professed duellist, who minded dirking a man no more than a genuine republican, and that he had been long enough in the country to become very expert in gouging. I could have got him killed outright for ten dollars, that being the usual rate in this country;* and people jump at a job so congenial to their habits and feelings. Besides, those who favour the profession for a livelihood have not much employment at present, as almost every genuine democrat prefers killing for himself. But upon the whole I concluded to let the fellow off, not being as yet sufficient of a republican to relish the killing of a man, either in person or by deputy.

The little Frenchman insisted upon knowing where I put up, no doubt with a view of consummating his plan of robbing me ; but I was resolved to keep that secret to myself. The more shy I

* Vide Quarterly, No. 58, Eng. Ed.

was, the more curious he became, so that I had no
other way of escaping his inquiries than leaving
the box, under pretence of getting some refresh-
ment.   The moment I got clear of him, I bolted
out of the house, and made the best of my way to
my lodgings. Just as I entered the door, however,
I heard the well-known sneeze, and glancing round
beheld the little Frenchman, and the communicative traveller, watching me from the opposite side
of the way.   The thing was now quite plain; no
one could mistake their object, and no time was to
be lost.   I determined to change my lodgings that
very night. So calling my worthy landlord out of
bed I paid his bill, took my portmanteau under
my arm, and proceeded to the city-hotel, where I
asked for a room, with a double lock to it, which
was shown me by the waiter, who by the way looked very much like a bandit ; and eyed me with a
most alarming expression of curiosity.

" Thank heaven," said I, after double-locking
the door, " I think I've distanced that little diabolical French cut-throat, and his accomplice, for
this night, at least." Carefully loading my pistols,
and placing them on a chair at the bed side, I sat
down to refresh my memory with the 58th number of the Quarterly.   After poring over the disgusting detail of the gougings, drinkings, roast-
ings, and impieties of republicanism, till my blood
ran cold, and my hair stood on end, I retired
to bed. Somehow or other I could not sleep. The
moment I attempted to close my eyes, visions of

horror arose, and my imagination teemed with the most appalling, vague, and indefinite dangers that seemed to beset me, I knew not where or how. As I lay thus under the influence of this providential restlessness, I heard in the next room that appalling and never to be forgotten sneeze, which never failed to announce the proximity of the little Frenchman. I started up, seized my pistols, and stood upon the defensive, determined to sell my life as dearly as possible. Presently some one tried the lock of my door, and I was just on the point of firing, when I heard a voice saying, " This is not the room, sir—you sleep in No. 40,"—and they passed onward.

What rendered my situation the more critical, was the circumstance of there being an additional door to my room, communicating with that of the French bandit, which I had not observed before. Cautiously approaching it with a pistol cocked in either hand, I found it locked indeed, but words cannot describe my sensations when I discovered the key was on the other side. However, a few moments restored me to the courage of desperation, and I ventured to peep through the key-hole, where I saw a sight that froze my blood. The little Frenchman, with his dark mahogany aspect, was sitting at a table with a case, not of pistols, but of razors, one of which he was carefully strapping. Ever and anon, as he tried it upon the palm of his hand, he observed to the communicative traveller : " Diable!—it will not do yet—'tis cer-

tainly made of lead." At last, however, it seemed to satisfy him, and he exclaimed with diabolical
exultation—"Ah, ha! he will do now—here is
an edge to cut off a man's head without his feeling
it." I instinctively drew my hand across my
neck to ascertain if my head was safe on my shoulders, and at that moment heard the voice of the
communicative traveller; "Had not you better
wait till to-morrow morning?" "Diable, no—
we shall not have time—now or never—I will not
spare a single hair a minute longer." A slight
movement followed this, and the little Frenchman
observed in reply to something which escaped me
in the bustle : "Do—do—one don't want any assist-
ance in these matters—I can do it very well myself." The bloody-minded villain, thought I,
he wants to have all the pleasure of killing me to
himself. Some one got up, moved towards the
door, tried the lock, and seemed just on the point
of opening it, when, thinking no time was to be
lost, I fired my pistol bang against the door. "Diable!" exclaimed the little Frenchman, "here is
our old friend, Monsieur John Bull, the agreeable
gentleman, come again. Somebody must be robbing him beyond doubt. Let us rescue him by all
means." They then attempted to unlock the door,
under pretence of rescue, but I cried out in a tone
of deep solemnity, "Stand off, villains! I have still
another loaded pistol, and the first of you that ap-
proaches is a dead man. Enter at your peril!"

9

By this time the whole house was in an uproar,
the lodgers bundled out of their rooms half dressed—the servant maids ran about squeaking, and
several ladies fell into fits.   I am safe enough for
the present, thought I, but nevertheless there is
nothing like being prepared; so I held fast my
loaded pistol, while the crowd, which at length
collected at my door, attracted by the smell of the
powder, called out to know what was the matter.
" There has been an attempt to rob and murder
me," answered I.   " By whom?" inquired the
voices.   " By a little mahogany-faced Frenchman
and a communicative traveller," answered I.
" Monsieur is under a grand mistake," cried the
little Frenchman.   " He was going to cut my
throat," cried I.   " I was going to cut off my
beard," answered the little Frenchman—upon
which the pure spirit of democracy burst out into
a loud laugh.   " He must have been dreaming,"
said one.   " He has had the nightmare," said
another.   " He must be drunk," cried a fourth.
" He must be mad," cried a fifth.   " By no means,"
cried the little Frenchman—" Monsieur has only
been reading the Quarterly Review, and is a little
afraid of the spirit of democracy.   He shall shoot
him one day with a silver bullet."   Hereupon
they all burst into a hideous democratic laugh,
which is ten times worse than a horse laugh, and
scampered off to bed leaving me at the mercy of
the two banditti.   Such is the protection afforded

a stranger, and particularly an Englishman, in this bundling, gouging, dirking, spitting, chewing, swearing, blaspheming den of democracy.*

* Vide No. 58.

CHAP. IX.

Author goes to the Police—Description of the magistrate—Mistake of his worship—Examination of the little Frenchman—Author quotes the Quarterly—Mr. Chichester—Dr. Thornton—Frenchman acquitted to the great delight of the Democrats, who all like the French, and why—Sympathy in favour of rogues here, and reasons for it—Philippic against democratic judges, magistrates, lawyers, and democrats in general—Moral air tainted, according to the Quarterly—Author leaves the city of abominations for fear of becoming a rogue, by the force of universal example—Turbulent spirit of democracy—Quarterly Review.

THE morning succeeding the attempt to rob and murder me, I inquired my way to the police-office, which I finally discovered at a cobbler's stall, in one of the filthiest streets of the whole city, called Pattypan-lane. I found his worship sitting on his bench, in a leather apron, most sedulously occupied in mending an old boot. On my informing him I had business, he looked down at my feet, very earnestly—"Hum! why your boots don't seem to want mending—but let us see." So he seized hold of my boot, and laid me sprawling on the floor, in attempting to pull it off. He then fell

into a passion with my boots, and swore the fellow
that made them so tight ought to be " dirked,"
the usual phrase for the punishment of slight offences among these humane republicans.

It was with some difficulty I made him understand my business was not with the cobbler, but
the magistrate. " Well, go on with your information," replied he, " while I finish my job ; I can
take a stitch while you tell your story." So he
fell to work lustily, while I proceeded to detail
the events of the last night. When I had done,
he looked at me for a moment, and then with the
true gravity and demeanour of a genuine republican magistrate, burst into a horse laugh, and took
into his mouth a huge quid of tobacco. " And you
are positive their intention was to rob and murder
you?" quoth the sage Minos. I offered to swear
to it, upon which he handed the book, and admi-
nistered the oath. " Very well, we must send
for these bloody-minded villains, and see what
they have to say for themselves. A little Frenchman, with a mahogany face, gold ear-rings, and
dimity breeches, say you? we must describe the
villain, as you don't know his name." On receiving satisfaction as to this point, he procured a warrant, which he signed with his cross, being una-
ble to write his name ; desired me to witness his
mark ; and sent off one of his apprentices to bring
the offenders.

In a few minutes he returned with the little
Frenchman, his companion, and almost all the lodg-

9*

ers at the city-hotel, landlord, waiters, and all.
His worship laid down his awl, and the examination began.

"What is your name?"

"Pierre François Louis Maximilian Joseph
Maria Gourgac d'Espagnac de Gomperville," answered the little bandit.

"A whole band of robbers, in the person of one
little Frenchman," observed his worship, turning
to his clerk, and directing him to write it down.
The clerk demurred to this, as to write it was quite
impossible.

"Well, then," said his worship, "write down
Hard name, and proceed. Whence came you,
where are you going, what is your business, and
how came you to put this gentleman in bodily fear
last night?"

"I came," replied the bandit, "from New-
Orleans, which, as Monsieur knows (making me
a low bow) is not far from Portsmouth, in Alabama. I am going to Charleston, to which place I
hope to have the pleasure of Monsieur's company,
(making me another low bow;) my business, it
seems, is principally to rob and murder Monsieur,
(another bow,) and I came to put him in bodily
fear, by reason of sharpening my razors at night,
which I generally do before I shave myself;"
making me another low bow, and offering his box.

"Hum!" quoth his worship, eying the little
Frenchman's stiff black beard, "A man with such
a brush under his nose might reasonably strap his

razors over night, I should think, without being
suspected of any other intent but to cut up his own
stubble field.   But what other proofs have you of
this intent to rob and murder, hey?"

   " My own conviction," answered I.

   " Aye! but a man's conviction is no proof of
guilt, except it be a conviction by judge and jury,"
answered the learned justice.

   " The word of a gentleman!"

   " Pooh! the word of a gentleman is no better
than the word of any other man.   Every man is a
gentleman in this free country," replied the democratic Solon.

   " Did they break into your room?"

   " No—but they tried the lock."

   " Did they actually offer you any violence, or
attempt to cut your throat?"

   " No—but the little Frenchman sharpened his
razors at me."

   " Have you any witnesses to prove the attempt?"

   " The circumstances are, of themselves, sufficient—besides, they have followed me all the way
from Portsmouth, and this is not the first time the
little Frenchman, and his accomplices, have made
the attempt."

   " Followed you!" quoth Solon; " travelling in
the same stages and steam-boats, and putting up at
the same houses, is what generally happens to people travelling the same route—this is no proof of
wicked intention."

The little Frenchman now appealed to the crowd of city-hotel people, who, beyond doubt, were all his accomplices, and who all testified that he had been there two days before I made my appearance, which the stupid cobbler-justice observed was proof that he had not followed me, at the same time hinting to the Frenchman, he had good grounds for an information against me for following *him!* Finding they were all in league together, I determined to overwhelm the justice, the clerk, the witnesses, and the culprits, by one single irresistible testimony. I took from my pocket the fifty-eighth number of the Quarterly, which I always carry about me; and turning to page three-hundred and fifty, seven, read in an audible voice as follows:*

" Mr. Chichester told him," (Mr. Faux,) " that ten dollars would procure the life and blood of any man in this country." Mr. Chichester also told me, that "he knew a party of whites who, last year, roasted to death before a large log fire one of their friends, because he refused to drink."†

" And who is Mr. Chichester?" said the ignoramus, who, it is plain, never reads the Quarterly.

"Mr. Chichester is a polished, gay, interesting gentleman, travelling in his own carriage from Kentucky to Virginia," replied I, reading in the Quarterly.‡ Again, sir, " Judge Waggoner, who

* Vide No. 58, *English copy.*　　　† Ditto.　　　‡ Ditto.

is a notorious hog-stealer, was recently accused, while sitting on the bench, by Major Hooker, the hunter, gouger, whipper, and nose-biter, of stealing many hogs, and being, although a judge, the greatest rogue in the United States."* Again, sir, we read from this same unquestionable authority, "Doctor Thornton,† of the post-office, observed to him that *this* city, like that of ancient Rome, was peopled with thieves and assassins, and that during his residence in it, he had found more villains than he had seen in all the world besides."

"And pray who is Doctor Thornton—is he in court?" cried this pious minister of justice.

"Doctor Thornton," replied I, "is a gentleman of character and learning—he has invented a new alphabet."

"Diable!" interrupted the little Frenchman—"'tis not the only thing he has invented I believe."

I continued without noticing the interruption—Dr. Thornton, sir, is an Englishman, and that is a sufficient warrant for all he says. I know, however, from the best authority, that by his eloquence he prevented the gallant Cockburn from burning the capitol and president's house during the late war."

"Diable!" again interrupted the little Frenchman, "am I to be convicted of murder upon the testimony of the goose whose cackling saved the capitol?"

Vide No. 58.   † Ditto

"But what do you intend by all this?" replied his worship petulantly, and casting a wishful eye at his old boot, as if he wanted to be stitching again.

"I mean, sir," replied I solemnly, "to prove by this testimony, that as ten dollars is the price of blood in this country, that as Judge Waggoner is a notorious hog-stealer, and that, as Doctor Thornton affirms, four cities are peopled by thieves and robbers, that in such a country, and among such a people, the mere sharpening of a razor at such an unreasonable hour, is sufficient presumptive proof, to hang half a dozen Frenchmen and democrats."

But the little Frenchman, who had by this time sent and suborned the president of a bank, and two or three directors, his accomplices no doubt, offered their testimony to prove that he was a person well known to them, of ample means and unblemished character, equally above the temptation as the suspicion of robbery or murder. Upon this, in spite of my own testimony, and the authority of the Quarterly, the precious cobbling justice dismissed my complaint, and apprized the little Frenchman that he might recover damages of me if he chose. But the little bandit had other objects in view, and after receiving the congratulations of all present, (for these people adore the French only because they take a little pains to be agreeable,) turned to me with a most diabolical smile, made me a low bow, offered his box, earnestly hoped he should have the pleasure of my agreeable company to Charleston, and assured me, upon his honour,

he would never attempt to cut my throat again
since he was born.

From this specimen of the mode of administering republican justice, and the character of the
judges, who are, for the most part, pig-stealers, and
never read the Quarterly, one may judge of the
chance an Englishman has of protection or redress.
Every body is in league against him; it is sufficient
for a man only to be accused of doing wrong, in
order to excite the universal sympathy in his favour.   The officers of the courts, the magistrates,
judges, lawyers, and spectators, all have a fellow-
feeling for a criminal, having all been, or expecting soon to be in a similar predicament, and the
accuser is thrice lucky, if he does not change places
with the accused.   The lawyers, who are most expert in snatching murderers from the gallows, are
certain to be made magistrates, and the most dexterous pig-stealer is predestined to be a judge of
pig-stealers.   The sheriff, not long since, was
obliged to hang his own nephew for the murder
of his mother, who was the sheriff's sister, as these
virtuous self-governing republicans thought it a
pity to hang a man for such a trifle, and not one
of them would tie the knot! The moral air is putrid, and even the most honest Englishman cannot
breathe it without his principles being tainted with
the plague of democracy.   Feeling this to be actually the case with myself, I determined to change
the air as soon as possible, and not caring to go
back again to the hotel, to meet the banditti, and

their accomplices, I desired my old landlord, the gentleman of colour, to go and pay for my lodgings, and bring my portmanteau down to the steam-boat, just then departing for the south. I embarked in her, shaking the dust off my feet, as I left this city of abominations, in which though I had staid but two days, I had seen more of the turbulent spirit of democracy than in all the world beside. No wonder, seeing " it is peopled by thieves and robbers ;" and the Quarterly affirms it to be the place where the " scum of all the earth"* is collected.

Vide No. 58, Eng. Ed.

CHAP. X.

Miraculous escape in crossing the East River to Jersey—Author
makes his will previously—Number of people at Communipaw on crutches—His fellow traveller, an Englishman, tells a
story accounting for it—Manner of keeping the Sabbath—Lit
tle Frenchman identified—Inhumanity of republicans—Drunken driver—Philosophical reasons why republicans must naturally be hard drinkers—Apostrophe in praise of oriental despotism, and abject poverty.

THE steam-boat in which I embarked, as stated
in the last chapter, conveyed us across the East
River to the Jersey shore, without bursting her
boiler, which was considered little less than a miracle, as there is scarcely a day passes without a
catastrophe of this kind, which is fatal to a dozen
or twenty people. Yet the people go on board
these vessels with as little hesitation as they would
enter their own doors. Indeed, their carelessness
of their own lives is equal to their disregard of
the lives of others, and they encounter the risk of
being scalded to death, with as little hesitation
as they feel in dirking an intimate friend, or burn-

ing him on a pile of logs for not drinking.* For
my part, I took the precaution previous to my em-
barkation, to settle my affairs and make my will.
It proved, however, unnecessary in this instance,
as we were safely landed in the city of Communipaw, the capital of that state.

The first thing that struck me in roaming about
here waiting for the stage, which was delayed for
the purpose of giving the driver time to get drunk,
was the vast proportion of people upon crutches.
Almost every person I met had lost his feet and
a part of his legs; some at the ancles, some at
the calves, and a few at the knee. On inquiring
of a person who was to be my fellow traveller
the cause of this singularity, he gave me the following details, than which nothing can more bril-
liantly illustrate the manner in which the Sabbath
is kept, or rather profaned, among " these bundling, gouging, spitting, swearing, dirking, drinking, blaspheming republicans."†

" You must know, sir," said my informant,
" that the people of this city and its neighbourhood,
are notorious all over the country for dancing.
Such is their fondness for the amusement, that they
don't know when to stop, and if it happens to be
Saturday night, they are pretty sure to dance till
day-light on Sunday morning, let what will happen. About three years ago there was a grand
ball given, in which the mayor, aldermen, and all

---

* Vide No. 58. Eng. Ed.   † Ditto. Eng. Ed.

the fashionable people of the town were present. Unluckily it happened to be Saturday night, and the company continued dancing till the clock struck twelve. But not a soul heard it, they were so busy in shuffling 'hoe corn' and 'dig potatoes,' and if they had, nobody would have abated a single shuffle. Just as the clock struck, there came in a little black gentleman, with gold ear-rings, a mahogany face, and dressed in a full suit of black, except that he wore dimity breeches."

" The little Frenchman, by Heaven!" exclaimed I.

" You shall hear anon," continued he. " The little black gentleman cut into a Scots reel without ceremony, and danced with such extraordinary vigour and agility, that every body seemed inspired. The young fellows threw off their coats first, then their waistcoats, and there is no knowing how much farther they might have proceeded had not good manners prevented. The buxom Dutch girls of Communipaw kicked up their heels, and gamboled with all the vivacity of young elephants, and bundling came to be very seriously contemplated. But it would have done your heart good to see the fiddler, a gentleman of colour, belonging to Squire Van Bommel, who gradually got his fiddle locked fast between his breast and chin, where he wedged it up with both knees, while his mouth gradually expanded from ear to ear, as he played Yankee Doodle as if the d——l was in him. The little black gentleman was the life and soul

of the party ; bowed to every body, danced with
every lady, complimented every body, offered his
box to every body, took snuff with every body, and
sneezed—"

"O! the little Frenchman," cried I, "I'll bet
a hundred pounds!"

"You shall hear," continued my companion.
"All was joy, laughter, capering, singing, bundling,
swearing, gouging, dirking, and hilarity, when
by degrees the young damsels and lads began to
find their bare feet coming to the floor, which reminded them it was time to stop dancing, But it
was too late now. There was a spell upon them,
and they continued to dance away by an irresistible impulse, till, by-and-by, first went the skin off
the soles of their feet, then the feet themselves.
Still they continued dancing, and the shorter their
legs grew, the higher they capered, and the faster
the fiddler played Yankee Doodle, the black gentleman vociferating all the while, in concert—

"Yankee doodle keep it up,
"Yankee doodle dandy ;
"Mind the music and the step,
"And with the *gals** be handy.

"But how did it happen," said I, "that the
black gentleman, alias the little Frenchman, did
not lose his feet and legs too?"

* This shows that even the devils don't speak good English
among these enlightened republicans.

" I have not said he didn't yet," replied my companion. " But, however, your suggestion is correct. He kept capering away without either feet or legs diminishing any more than if they had been of steel. But no wonder, as you will find in the sequel. The company continued to caper and jig it, till the legs of many were entirely danced away, and it has been asserted that the fiddler's chin was more than half gone. Nay, there have been those who do not scruple to affirm that several heads, without either feet, legs, or body at all, were seen cutting pigeon wings and taking the partridge run with all the alacrity imaginable. But of this there is some contrariety of opinion.

" Certain it is that the dancing continued with unabated vigour, the little black gentleman still setting the example, and the fiddler, having entirely wore out his fiddle-strings, was sawing away tooth and nail upon the edge of his fiddle. And here I must remark a most extraordinary circumstance, which is that the longer they danced, the shorter they grew, by reason of their wear and tear of feet, legs, &c., so that beyond all doubt had they danced much longer, there would have been nothing left of them, not even the hair of their heads. Luckily, however, an old one-eyed rooster, who sat upon one leg on a pole that lay across the crotches of two trees, and where they generally hung up their pigs by the hinder legs—"

10*

"What," interrupted I, "do they hang pigs in this country?"

"Yes," replied my companion, with a sigh. "But the less we say about that the better. You will hardly believe it, but they hang them up with their heads downwards;" and thereupon he took out his handkerchief and wiped his eyes. Well may you blush and weep over the inhumanity of your countrymen, thought I. The Quarterly shall hear of this.

"But," resumed my companion in a hurried manner, as if anxious to direct my attention from this horrible cruelty, "let us go back to the old rooster, who about daylight clapped his wings and crowed so loud that you might have heard him across the river. No sooner had the little black gentleman heard the clapping and crowing, than he made one bound up the chimney, without making his bow to the company, or taking leave of six ladies to whom he had engaged himself to be married the next morning. He was heard to sneeze as he ascended the chimney, which thereupon burst with a terrible explosion of red hot bricks, which flew about in the sky like great fire-flies, hissing like serpents. This was succeeded by a shower of flour of brimstone, which cured all the people thereabouts of the Scots fiddle. The fiddler was found two days afterwards with his head buried in a salt marsh near Communipaw, and his stumps dancing in the air scraping Yankee Doodle like a devil incarnate. The dancers all ran home."

"What," said I, "without their legs—how could that be?"

"I can't say," replied he, "but run they did as fast as legs could carry them, although, as you have ocular demonstration, they must have done it without legs. To conclude, the doctors hearing of this catastrophe, came over in shoals from New-York, thinking they would have some profitable job, but, to their great mortification, found all their stumps perfectly healed by what seemed to be the application of a red hot iron, so that they paid their ferriage across the river and ran the risk of the bursting of the boiler for nothing. It is observed that the dancers all continue to smell of brimstone to this day. The windows of the house in which the dance took place, sometimes, particularly during storms of thunder and lightning at night, seem as if the whole was on fire, and some have said they saw the little black gentleman dancing there surrounded by old women on broomsticks. This is doubtful; but certain it is that the old one-eyed rooster was killed the following christmas night in a battle royal between the Harsimusites and the Hobokenites, in which the former were worsted."

"I suppose," said I, "this cured them of dancing on Sunday mornings?"

"Not in the least," replied he. "These very people you see upon crutches, are eternally jigging it and frisking their tails. You shall see."

So he began whistling Yankee Doodle, and in

the space of five minutes, at least thirty people, without a single leg between them, gathered round us dancing most incontinently. I turned in disgust from this incorrigible race of impious republicans, whom the loss of legs cannot restrain from a breach of the Sabbath, and who persevere in their enormities even in despite of miracles, as the Quarterly says. But my reflections were interrupted by the arrival of the stage, the driver being at length " prime bang up," that is to say, as drunk as a lord.

In the course of my travels, I have often reflected on the causes of that universal and inveterate propensity to drunkenness, which is the characteristic of this people, and the result is, that it is another of the delectable offspring of the turbulent spirit of democracy. Nothing is more certain than that a people will be restrained in proportion to the restraints under which they labour. In proportion to the freedom they enjoy, will be the freedom of their indulgences. It is only by taking away the freedom of action, and the means of obtaining these indulgences, that you can make the vulgar either tolerably religious, or decently moral. The right of self-government is another word for the freedom from all moral and religious restraints, and it is a clear deduction to say, that a man who don't honour the king will seldom fear his Maker. Again—the consciousness of freedom generates among the vulgar, and all free people may be called vulgar, a certain degree of impudence, a hardy confidence which carries a man above those salutary restraints which the opinion and influence of society impose upon mankind. Lastly, where a large portion of the people can earn a superfluity, above the wants of themselves and families, they will be almost certain to devote their substance to riot and debauchery.

It is thus with this wretched spawn of democracy. Boasting, as they do, of the right of making their own laws, they naturally claim and exercise the right of breaking them whenever they please. Being free from the salutary restraints of European, and Oriental despotism, they naturally throw off all restraint; having plenty of money beyond the necessary wants of life, they naturally become wasteful; and feeling themselves equal to any and every man they meet, they naturally and inevitably become insolent and intemperate. It would be considered a proof of a most mean and abject spirit, for a genuine republican to show his respect for any society whatever, by behaving with decency and keeping himself sober.

Such being the case, happy thrice happy are those who have no voice in making the laws, for they will be the more likely to obey them. Happy, and four times happy are they, who never taste the unhallowed cup of freedom, for they will not be ruined by the absence of all restraints. Happy, and six times happy, are the people who have no taste of that fatal equality which generates a vulgar confidence that disdains all subserviency to rank, dress, and equipage—and happy above all happy people are those, who, being stinted in the means of procuring even the necessaries of life, will never be able to indulge in enervating pleasures, or the excesses of intemperance.

CHAP. XI.

UNDER the protection of that Providence, which
is said to take the special guardianship of drunken
stage drivers, we proceeded on, over one of the
most rocky, rutty, and infamous roads I ever
travelled. The spirit of democracy disdains to
pay any regard to the laws for mending roads, it
being an approved maxim, that the best way to
mend the roads is to let them mend themselves.
Yet notwithstanding all this, there are turnpike
gates every two or three miles, especially in New-
England, and the other southern states, where
they take enormous toll of all strangers, especially

Englishmen, who being distinguished by a certain air of nobility, which causes them to be all taken for *my lords* by the French and Italians, are easily detected by these cunning Yankees.

But notwithstanding the situation of the driver, and the roughness of the roads, we proceeded on without any accident, and rather more pleasantly than usual. My companion turned out to be an Englishman, which, in truth, I had not suspected before, though I might have known it by his speaking such pure English, and was rather inclined to be shy of his attentions. But the moment he informed me he was a native of Yorkshire, my suspicions vanished, for an Englishman may be trusted all the world over, all the world knows. By degrees we became sociable, for I saw he was a man of education and discernment, by his always addressing me as my lord. One inquiry led to another, and at length he told me his story, which I shall set down word for word, as a warning to my simple, credulous countrymen, who are allured to this land of promise by the modern Moses of transatlantic speculation, as the Quarterly says.

" I was very well hoff at ome," said he, " aving a good farm, with comfortable hout-ouses, and plenty of stock, say five undred Norfolk sheep, forty or fifty Bakewell cows, and two bulls of the Tees-water breed. But somecow hor hother, I went beindand every year. The rents hi paid to keep hup the dignity of the nobleman, my landlord— the taxes hi paid to support the splendours of the

king, God bless him—the tithes hi paid for sup-
porting the established church, without which
hevery body knows there can be no religion—and
the poor rates which hi paid to keep hup that state
of poverty and dependence, without which no people can be virtuous and appy—hall these put together, pulled me down every year by little and
little. But hall these were has nothing compared
to certain hother matters. The cost of maintaining hold England, in the igh latitude of the bulwark of religion, fell ard upon me—then hafter
that, the putting down of Bonaparte, and securing
the liberties hoff Heurope, fleeced me pretty and-
somely. But hi might ave got hover these, but
for a plentiful arvest, which coming on the back
of hall the rest, stripped me of the fruits of my
labours, and brought me pretty deeply hin debt.

"Habout this time, Satan, who halways his hat
ha man's helbows, hin time hof distress, threw hin
my way that mischievous radical Birkbeck's book
habout the Henglish Prairie, which seduced me
hinto the hidea of selling hoff my hall and hemi-
grating to Hamerrykey."

"Did you ever read the Quarterly?" said I.

"Nay—but hi have hattended the quarter ses-
sions pretty regularly for many years past," replied he.

"Ah! what a pity—what a pity," said I—"if
you had only read the Quarterly you'd never have
come to this land of gouging, dirking, bundling,
and guessing."

11

" I guess not," quoth he, and went on with his story.

" Hi was ha saying, that Birkbeck's book fell hin my way, hand gave such ha seducing picture of the prairie, that hi sold hoff, and all the stock hi ad saved, from the landlord, the king, the church, the paupers, the bulwark of religion, the seeuring hof the liberties hof Heurope, hand the plentiful arvest. The proceeds hi turned into guineas, hand quilted them into the waistband hof my breeches."

I shall here give the remainder of his narrative in Yankee English, for really I have been long enough here to find the writing of pure English rather awkward.

" I embarked," continued my companion, " for Boston, which, I learned from a gentleman who told me he superintended the geography of the Quarterly Review, was close by English Prairie. On landing there, which I did without being ship-wrecked, although the vessel was a Yankee, and the captain and crew drunk all the voyage, the first thing I did was to ask how far it was to English Prairie? I was in a hurry, and wanted to get there before night. The landlord, of whom I inquired, after scratching his head some time, replied :—

" English Prairie—are you going there?"

" Yes—I expect to be there before dark."

" Do you?—Why then I guess you mean to travel in a balloon—don't you?"

" Dam'me, sir," replied I, " do you mean to hoax me?"

" Hoax—what's that?"

" I say quiz me."

" Quiz—what's that?"

" I say," replied I, " can you tell me how far it is to English Prairie?"

" Why, if you really wish to know—I can't say exactly, for I never was there—but I should guess it can't be less than twelve hundred miles, or thereabouts."

" Twelve hundred d——ls," cried I.

" No, not devils," said Jonathan, " but miles; and devilish long miles, I reckon."

" Looking about, I saw a map of the states, which, by the way, is a usual thing all over this country, the people being eternally travelling by maps.   On examination, I found, to my utter astonishment, that brother Jonathan was right.   I might as well have gone to English Prairie by way of the Cape of Good Hope, as Boston.   This was one of the first blessed effects of Birkbeck's book. On referring to it, I found indeed that he had stated the distance and the route, but it had escaped my notice, confound him.

" However, since I had come so far, I thought I would not go back with a flea in my ear, and so I determined to seek the distant land of promise "

" What a pity—what a pity," interrupted I, " you never read the Quarterly."

" I am determind to read nothing else from this

time forward—at least if I can procure a copy,"
replied he, upon which I handed him the English
copy of the fifty-eighth number, telling him it was
heartily at his service during the time we travelled together. He thanked me, called me my lord
three times, and proceeded.

"It would be tedious to give an account of the
difficulties, mortifications, insults, dangers, and
scrapes I encountered in my journey. I was four
times robbed of all I had in the world. I was six
times gouged, eight times dirked, and several
times roasted at a log fire. before I arrived at English Prairie. By the blessing of Providence, however, I got there at last, and much good did it do
me. My first disappointment in not meeting the
back country close by the sea shore, was nothing to
those I encountered here. Instead of finding the back-
woods all cleared away, comfortable houses, barns
fences, hedges, ditches, school-houses, churches,
bishops, noblemen, and kings, I found a parcel of rude, hard-working men, with axes on one
shoulder, and guns on the other. The first thing
they told me was to cut down the trees, which
were generally about the size of a hogshead. I
laid close siege to one for three days, and found
by a pretty clear deduction, that it would take five
days more to bring it to the earth. I then count-
ed the trees upon my plantation, and found that if
I lived to the age of Methusaleh, I might possibly
clear a place big enough for a potato patch.

"My next inquiry was, as to how they procured their food. 'You must go into the woods,' said a fellow in a hunting shirt and moccasons, 'there is plenty of deer and wild turkeys.' 'But I never fired a gun in my life,' answered I. 'Then what the d——l sent you here?' cried he, at the same time gouging out one of my eyes, I suppose to qualify me to take aim with proper accuracy. Not being able to cut down trees, or shoot deer and wild turkeys, I was in a fair way of starving. I resolved, for the last resort, the poor-house.— But in this barbarous place, there was no poor-house to be found. I then applied to my good neighbour, who had favoured me by gouging out one eye, for a piece of venison. He gave me a saddle and a wild turkey, saying, at the same time, in the most unfeeling manner, 'every body works here friend, and every man provides for himself. Don't come again begging.' Whereupon he goug-ed out another eye. Shortly after he came to in-vite me to a Barbacue, as it is called, which is a sort of fea t, where they generally serve up a ba-ked Indian or two, whom they have hunted and shot in the course of the morning. I expressed my abhorrence of this cannibal feast, and declined go-ing, upon which he gouged out another eye, and swore he'd not leave a single eye in my head if I did'nt go. Thinking it better to eat Indians than be blind, I signified my consent, and accompanied this hospitable person.

"It would be impossible to describe this feast. Suffice it to say, that it ended in a scene of drunk-

11*

enness and bloodshed, that was enough to sicken a
pirate or a republican. The conclusion was, that
every soul present was either murdered or left in-
sensible on the ground—after which they threw
me upon a log-fire, and burnt me to a cinder, because I wouldn't drink " confusion to the Holy
Alliance." My misfortunes did not end here; in
one night they robbed me of twenty or thirty
pigs, it being their maxim that it is more convenient to steal than buy, which constitutes the quin-
tessence of republican ethics,* as the Quarterly
says. I was on my way to the judge, to complain
of this theft, when I met my gouging friend, to
whom I related my misfortune. He burst into a
horse-laugh, which resolved itself into a yell, and
tapered off with the Indian war-whoop. When
he had done, he solemnly assured me that my pigs
were now in the judge's pen; that his honour was
the most noted pig-stealer in the place, and had
been elevated to the bench solely on that account.
it being shrewdly suspected that he would let off
all the pig-stealers, who constitute the majority of
the people, from a fellow feeling. ' It is of no use,
said he, ' to go to the judge. The only remedy
you have is to try and steal somebody else's pigs.
If you can rob the judge, you will get his place to
a certainty.' I expressed an abhorrence of this
mode of righting myself; upon which he swore I
had reflected upon the native character, and gouged
out one of my eyes.

    " Soon after, it was buzzed about that I had been

* Vide No. 58. Eng. ed.

on the point of appealing to the laws for redress,
and moreover demurred to the Indian law of reta-
liation, the only law in force at English Prairie.
For these heinous offences, I was informed private-
ly, by a worthy English settler, who had been like
me seduced by Mr. Birkbeck, that they had hired
a man to dirk me for ten dollars, the usual price of
blood in this country, as Mr. Chichester says.*
Thinking it high time to take care of myself, I
sold my land at less than half price, to the worthy
English settler, and made off, with all the speed in
my power, for a civilized Christian land.   I had
almost forgot to tell you, that just on the skirt of
the Prairie, I met a party of ladies, belonging to
the settlement, who roasted me alive, at a log-fire.
It was a mercy that I escaped."

"Pray," said I, when he had finished, "do they
ever read the Quarterly at English Prairie?"

"The Quarterly! Lord bless you—they read
nothing but Tom Paine.   I never saw any other
book in all the Western country."

"Not read the Quarterly!" exclaimed I—"Ah,
that accounts for their barbarity."

We now entered a dense, smoky, drizzling atmosphere, which succeeded so suddenly to a bright
cloudless day, that we did not know what to make
of it.   As we proceeded, the density and drizzling
increased, so that it became impossible to distinguish the road, which, however, was of the less
consequence, as our driver had been for some time
nodding on his seat fast asleep.   Suddenly the

* Vide No. 58. Eng. ed.

horses stopped of themselves, at what after a considerable degree of peering about, I discovered to
be a house, on the long piazza of which were seated an immense number of fat fellows, with broad-
brimmed hats, smoking and spitting in the true
republican style, that is to say, in every one's faces.*
This circumstance accounted for the smoky and
drizzling atmosphere, which extended upwards of
three miles in circumference, and obscured the
whole city, which was called Communipaw. Such
is the extent of this practice of smoking tobacco,
that at a certain period of the year, during the autumn, when the people of the country have finished gathering in the products of their fields, and
their leisure time comes, they commence a smoking festival, in which every man, woman, and
child partakes. This festival lasts five or six weeks,
during which time the atmosphere throughout the
whole extent of the country becomes so hazy, and
obscure, that they are obliged to burn candles all
day, and a perpetual drizzling prevails, owing to
the unseemly habit of spitting, which all our English travellers have heretofore noticed among
these immaculate republicans. This season is called the Indian summer, and the people pretend to
ascribe it to the Indian custom of burning the
long grass of the immense Prairies in the west. But
the above is the true solution, I can assure my
readers.

Being resolved not to sit still in the stage, and
be spitten to death, for all the stages here are

* Vide Quarterly.

without covering, for the convenience of letting in
the rain, I jumped out and sheltered myself under
a neighbouring shed. By-and-by I heard the driver calling for his passengers, but I was determined
not to be hurried, and took no notice of his insolence. Presently I heard the cracking of the whip
and the rumbling of the wheels, when I thought to
myself I had better condescend to call and stop him.
Accordingly I sallied forth in the fog and drizzle,
calling out to stop as loud as I could bawl, and
running every now and then against a long pipe,
invisible in the obscurity. The sound of the wheels
served as a sort of guide through the cimmerian
shades ; but as ill luck would have it, just as I
came up with the stage, which I afterwards discovered had been stopped at the pressing instances of
my companion, I unfortunately fell into a ditch by
the road side, where I was grievously annoyed by
a concert of frogs, which mistaking me, I suppose,
for king Log, jumped upon me, and sung with
true republican melody.

" You democratic rascal," cried I to the driver,
" what business had you to go off without me ?"

" Why," replied the impudent scoundrel, " I
thought you had gone off without me. I hollowed
till my throat was so dry, that I was obliged to
call for a pint of whiskey to whet my whistle."

" But why didn't you stop, when I called ?"

" Why," replied the villain, " it was so foggy
I couldn't see which way the sound came from."

Upon this I was going to thrash him soundly for his insolence, when my companion advised me not. ' If you attempt it,' said he, ' ten to one you will lose both eyes, and the better part of your nose, for this fellow has exactly the look of a first-rate gouger.' I thereupon determined to put up with the affair, considering it a portion of that series of imposition, impudence, rudeness, and barbarity which constitutes the basis of the republican character.*

It is in truth impossible to be in this country a day without being thoroughly convinced of the fact, that the possession of freedom necessarily brings with it an overwhelming mass of ignorance, corruption, and barbarity.† This position is supported by the history of the world, and the example of all nations. The republics of Greece were little better than nests of barbarous libertines, as is proved by the licentious freedoms which Terence, and other comic writers, took with persons in authority at Athens ; their banishment of Grotius, and others, the most illustrious of their citizens. Their whole claim to learning consisted in being able to talk Greek ; and as to their excellence in the mechanical arts, such as sculpture and painting, they are far excelled by the manufactories of Birmingham and Sheffield, in skill, and by the pot-bakers of Staffordshire, in the art of painting. And how *can* it be otherwise, since it is morally impossible it *should* be otherwise in all free states.

* Vide Quarterly, No. 58, Eng. Ed.   † Ditto.

The great and universal stimulus to excellence of every kind, is a desire to please those above us. To the applauses of our equals we are indifferent, and the admiration of our inferiors only excites our contempt. A conquering general, followed by thousands of people shouting at his heels, throwing up their caps, and giving way to all the extravagances of vulgar enthusiasm, looks with indifference at the crowd, and sighs for the glorious privilege of being permitted to kneel at the footstool of his most august and gracious sovereign, and to kiss his hand. What is the applause and admiration of a whole people compared to being made a knight companion of Bath, and called sir? This noble desire to please the great, is founded on the conviction, that they alone are worth pleasing, because they only have the power of rewarding. It is by their approbation and influence alone, that merit can hope to attain to its reward in the possession of titles, the only object of honourable ambition ; and of wealth, the sole means of rational enjoyment.

But where there is no distinction of rank, and all men are equal, the universal stimulus is wanting. There is nobody to please worth pleasing, because there are no kings, or nobility, whose smile alone confers distinction ; and there is nothing worth asking our genius to attain, because there are neither titles, ribbons, nor pensions. Hence arises the lamentable lack of illustrious men, in ancient as well as modern republics, and the deplorable contrast they exhibit compared with the splendours of Sesostris, Xerxes, Alaric, and prince Esterhazy in his diamond coat.   It is unnecessary to multiply examples to prove that the human mind can never attain to its highest elevation in a republic, and that as the United States never have, so it is probable they never will produce a truly great man until their government has titles, pensions, and ribbons to bestow.

The same causes lie at the root of that coarseness, rudeness, and forwardness of manner, for which these immaculate republicans (as the Quarterly says*) are so infamously distinguished.   All the regulations of polite life, and all refinements of manners, are the result of imitation, and people never think of imitating their equals, much less their inferiors.   Now nothing can be clearer than that where all are equal, as in this immaculate republic, there can be nobody to be imitated, and consequently no refinement of manners, and no judicious perception of what is due to themselves or to others.   People unacquainted with the divine majesty of a king, the splendours of his nobility, and the wealth of his bishops, cannot possibly have any proper idea of the dignity of human nature.   Having no standard among them, it is plain they must degenerate into barbarism, merely for want of a proper example.   That awe which seizes the mind in the presence of a

Vide Quarterly, No. 58, Eng. ed.

king, runs through all the gradations of life. In the presence of a nobleman, it becomes a due respect for rank—in that of a bishop, a proper sense of religion—and finally, by degrees, it settles down into that refined sentiment of politeness, which proportions its attentions to the dress, equipage, and general appearance of wealth a man exhibits to the world.

Here, on the contrary, where the vulgar system of equality extends to all classes, there exists a certain low emulation of the pretensions of every man who carries any appearance of superiority or holds himself aloof from the crowd. If he does not sit at table with tag, rag, and bobtail, and condescend to sleep three in a bed with any body the landlord pleases to select for his companions, he may reckon himself fortunate in escaping without the loss of an eye and a piece of his nose. An instance of this barbarous antipathy to broad-cloth coats occurred in the steam-boat, coming from Boston, which I omitted to notice at the time. I was dressed in a blue frock of Shepherd's best regent cloth, handsomely embroidered, and every thing else in the first London style, leaning over the side railing, when I felt some one almost touch my elbow. On turning round, there was a fellow in a gray suit of domestic manufacture, a half-worn hat that smacked of the last century, and shoes with soles at least an inch thick. If the truth was known, I verily believe he wore hob-nails in them. I gave him a look which would have sent

a peasant in any civilized country, about his business in a hurry.   But the creature remained
hanging over the railing, close at my elbow, and
on our passing a fir-built vessel with a bit of striped bunting at her mast-head, had the impudence to
speak to me.   "That I believe is Old Ironsides,"
said he.   I looked at him with a vacant stare, and
said nothing.   "I was saying," resumed the homespun creature, "that ship is the United States fri-
gate Constitution.   What a fine old ship!"—and
then his eyes sparkled most intolerably.   I looked at him with my quizzing glass, dropt my under
lip, and turned on my heel, without taking any
further notice of him or Old Ironsides, and walked
to another part of the boat.   In about half a minute
he followed me.

"Pray, sir," said he, "have you the misfortune
to be deaf?"   No answer.

"Are you dumb, sir?"   No answer, but a persevering reconnoitre through the quizzing glass.

"If you can neither speak nor hear, may be you
can feel," said the turbulent spawn of democracy,
raising his fist which was luckily arrested by the
little Frenchman, who, I suppose, was resolved that
nobody should murder me but himself.   "Diable!" cried the little man, "what is the matter—
what has Monsieur John Bull done, that you will
knock him down, eh?"   A Frenchman, somehow
or other, can do any thing with barbarians.   The
homespun monster dropped his huge paw, and
resumed a perfect good humour.

" I am wrong," said he, " because he is a stranger I perceive. Had he been one of my own countrymen, I would have *licked* him for his ill manners."

" Why, what did Monsieur do?" asked the little Frenchman.

" I spoke to him twice, and he would not answer me. It is the duty of every gentleman to answer a civil question. He was a stranger and alone, and I thought I would speak to him."

" Diable !" said the little man, " don't you know this is the great Monsieur John Bull, the bulwark of religion, the grand restorer of the liberties of Europe, who gained the battle of Waterloo all by himself, and who is the most learned, polite, and refined gentleman, in the whole world? Eh bien—it is lucky he did not look you stone dead. Don't you see his coat cost ten times as much as yours ?—Diable ! it was great courage to speak to him once, much more twice."

Here all the company burst into a coarse republican laugh, I could never tell at what, and the homespun monster departed with something on his tongue which sounded very much like "a dumbfounded potato." From this little anecdote the reader may form some faint idea of the gross freedom which pervades the manners of these republicans, who pay no more respect to regent's cloth, than they would to the regent himself.

CHAP. XII.

AFTER travelling all day over rough roads, and
through a dreary, barren wilderness, which is,
however, considered one of the best peopled and
best cultivated parts of the country, and where
every body was astonished to hear me speak English, we arrived late in the evening at Louisville,
the capital of the state of Tennessee. In walking
up from the stage-coach to the inn, I stumbled over
something, and what was my horror at discover-
ing a dead body weltering in blood! A little way
further on, I stumbled over another, and in this

way encountered six or seven, in less than the
space of thirty yards. Inquiring the cause of their
deaths, and the reason of their exposure in this
manner, the landlord seemed at a loss to understand me for a few minutes, which I ascribed to
my speaking pure English. After a little reflection, however, he seemed to recollect himself.

"O—ay—yes—I recollect—we had a *blow out*
here last Sunday, and half a dozen troublesome
fellows, they call justices, were done for by the
brave *rowdies*.* They won't interrupt sport again
I guess."

I turned sick at the barbarous indifference of
this immaculate republican, and asked him why
they suffered these bodies to remain thus without
burial. "O, we let them lie there as a warning
to our meddlesome magistrates, how they interrupt gentlemanly sports again. We were just
roasting a John Bull for not drinking his allowance of whiskey, when these gentry thought proper to interfere, but we soon did their business."
I may as well remark here once for all, that if I
make these republicans talk good English in my
journal, it is only because it is utterly impossible
to reduce their jargon to writing, and if it were,
no civilized reader could possibly understand it.
There is not a being living, who is a native of the
states, that can talk or write English.

I designed to question mine host still farther on
this matter, but just at the moment there was a

* Vide Quarterly.

12*

great uproar in an adjoining room, accompanied by cries of murder, upon which he hurried away "to see the sport," as he was pleased to term it. This sport, as I afterwards learned, consisted in a promising young republican of about seventeen, attempting to gouge his father, who had refused to call for another mint julep. My companion, who happened to look in, attempted to interfere, but narrowly escaped losing one, if not both his eyes, by the hands of the old gentleman, (every body is a gentleman here) who caned him for his impertinent interference, patting the promising youth on the head, and swearing he would turn out a true republican. Not content with a single julep, he called for a whole gallon, and they both got lovingly drunk together. Such, indeed, is the rage for mint juleps here, that nobody will buy a farm at any price unless it produces plenty of mint.

Reflecting on the barbarous indifference to life which characterizes these republicans,* I did not know but they might take it into their heads to kill me, and therefore proposed to my companion, the worthy emigrant, that we should sleep in the same room that night, for mutual comfort and protection. He seemed delighted with the proposal, and we accordingly, after supper, adjourned to a double-bedded room, the door of which we locked, my friend putting the key into his pocket for safety. He then took out the fifty-eighth number of the Quarterly and began to read the review of Faux's celebrated tour in America, which he said he could

* Vide Quarterly.

almost swear he had written himself, so exactly
did it tally with his own observation and experience

"And do the judges actually steal pigs?" inquired I. "Pigs!" answered my friend, "ay,
and every thing else they can lay their hands on.
It is a common thing for them to summon a man
before them, in order to insure his absence from
home, that they may have an opportunity of robbing his pig-sty without interruption."*

"And they take bribes too, I suppose?"

"You may say that," replied he. "There is
not a judge in the whole country that can resist a
pig or two. But it is seldom so high a bribe is
offered, except when a man wants to be acquitted
of two or three murders. The most common dou-
ceur is a paper of pins, and for this you may get a
decision which will entitle you to a thousand or
two acres of the best land in the world. You will
have to kill half a dozen *squatters* in order to get
possession, but this is considered a mere trifle."

"And were you not jesting when you talked
about their burning people on a log fire, when
they refuse to drink?"

"Not in the least," said he; "I solemnly assure
you that nothing is more common than such a frolic.
I knew several instances of fathers serving their own
children, and boys their own fathers, in this manner, during my stay at English Prairie, and it is
certain the custom is common in all the states."

Just at this instant a most poignant smell pervad-
ed our room, like that which accompanies the broil-

* Vide Quarterly.

ing of a rasher of bacon on the coals. My friend snuffed up the savoury effusion, and exclaimed,

" There !—they are at it now, I'll bet a thousand pounds. They're broiling some poor fellow to a certainty."*

" 'Tis bacon," said I.

" 'Tis a man," said he. " I can swear to the smell. I've had too much experience to be mistaken." And thereupon he began reading the fifty-eighth number of the Quarterly again with tears in his eyes.

It now waxed late in the night. The uproar of the inn gradually died away, the smell of the broiled republican subsided, and nothing was now heard save the owl, the whippoor-will, the bullfrog, the wolf, the watch-dog, and the sonorous tuning of many a vocal nose, chaunting sweet hallelujahs to the pure spirit of democracy. The Americans are, in truth, the greatest snorers in the world, which is doubtless owing to their all sleeping with their mouths wide open. I was puzzled to account for this habit, until Dr. Thornton afterwards assured me they slept with their mouths wide open for the convenience of swallowing a mint julep, which was always poured down their throats before they awoke in the morning, to keep them from getting the intermitting fever. Late as it was, I felt no inclination to sleep. I looked out of the window, and by the light of the moon could distinguish the bodies of the unfortunate magistrates, their pale faces turned upwards, and

* Vide Quarterly.

their white teeth shining in the silvery ray. Presently I saw a man cautiously stealing along towards the piggery, which is always in one corner of the kitchen, for the sake of security. He disappeared through the kitchen window; in a few moments a musket was fired, and I heard no more of the matter. The next morning all was explained. It was a neighbouring judge, who feeling an inclination for one of mine host's fat porkers, invaded his pig-sty that night. But to use the landlord's choice phrase, " he got his bitters,"—that is to say, he was shot through the head by mine host, who was on the watch, and I saw his body lying with the rest the next day.

Still sleep fled from my eyes, " the *innocent* sleep," for it could not exist amid these republican horrors. My companion grew more and more ardent in his persuasions for me to go to bed. "We will take turns to watch, and I will begin—Have you any arms? give them to me." I handed him my pistols, and at length overcome by his persuasions went to bed. It was long ere I could compose myself to rest; but at length the fatigues of the day gradually overpowered my apprehensions and I fell asleep. How long I slept I know not, but I was disturbed by something rummaging under my pillow, where I had placed my watch and pocket-book. The lights were all out, and I could see nothing; but thinking the little Frenchman was certainly come again, I called out " murder," as loud as I could, and thereupon heard the door

open, and somebody run off down the passage, as
fast as possible. Presently mine host, and several
other persons, came into the room with lights, and
inquired what was the matter?

" There has been an attempt to rob and murder
me," replied I.

" Well, what of that?" replied mine host—
" You need not have made such an infernal uproar,
and disturbed the whole house about nothing."

" Nothing! do you call robbing and murdering
a man nothing?"

" Yes," replied he, " just next to nothing. I
have known a dozen people robbed and murdered
in this house, with less noise than the stirring of a
mouser. But let us see if you have lost any thing?"

On examination, I found my watch and pocket-
book, which I had placed under my pillow, safe ;
but my pockets were rifled, and my pistols mis-
sing, together with the fifty-eighth number of the
Quarterly.

" But where is your companion?" asked some
one.   " Far enough from hence, by this time, I'll
warrant you ;" said mine host.

" What d'ye mean by that ?" said I.

" I mean that he has got your purse and pistols,
and you won't see him again in a hurry. The moment he came into the house last night, I knew
him for the English swindler, who broke jail last
spring."

" And why didn't you tell me he was a swin
dler?" said I indignantly.

" Why, to say the truth, I took you for another. Such pointers generally hunt in couples. Besides, there is so little difference among us genuine republicans, between an honest man and a swindler, that the distinction is not worth pointing out."

" I shall go to the justice and lay an information," said I.

" You needn't give yourself the trouble," replied mine host carelessly ; " there was but one justice left in all this county, and him I shot last night for making free with my pig-sty."

" O, liberty !" ejaculated I, in the bitterness of my heart, " thou art but a name—or rather thou art a name for all that degrades and disgraces human nature. Well may the Quarterly"—Here my soliloquy was cut short by the blowing of the driver's tin trumpet, the signal for departure, and what further I would have said must remain a secret to posterity for ever.

The disappointed emigrant from English Prairie did not make his appearance, and I pursued my journey, wrapt in solitary reflections. Insensibly I fell into a train of thought which led to an inquiry into the extraordinary paradox, that a country like this, destitute of every virtue, and devoid of every attraction under heaven,* should thus have imposed upon the whole world (except the Quarterly Reviewers) and lured from all parts of Christendom, crowds of emigrants, who, tired as it would seem, of the calm and happy security of legitimate governments, have sought misery and

* Vide Quarterly.

disappointment in these barbarous wilds. But mankind, thought I, have ever been the dupes of boastful pretension, and arrogant assumptions of superiority. The credulity of ignorance is unbounded; and when we revert to the belief even of sages and philosophers; the errors of Galileo and Copernicus, with regard to the great system of the universe, the blunders of Newton, and the follies of Philopoemen, it were hardly just to blame the errors of the common people. It is, therefore, excusable in the peasantry of distant countries, that they should be thus seduced by thousands, to leave their homes, by the impudent falsehoods every day palmed upon them by Mr. Birkbeck, and other retailers of radical trash.

But there is one thing which puzzled me at first. Notwithstanding the disappointments of these poor people, their being gouged, dirked, roasted, and having their pigs stolen by the judges; their being regulated and rowdied, and obliged to cut down trees as big round as a hogshead—notwithstanding there is neither law, gospel, decency, or morality in the whole country, and that no honest person can possibly live in it; notwithstanding that every emigrant, without exception,* is sighing ready to break his heart, to get home; notwithstanding all this, I say it is a remarkable fact, that not one in a thousand ever goes home again! They actually seem to be fascinated to the spot, by the charm of

* Vide No. 58, Eng. ed.

misery and despair, like the bird which flies into
the jaws of the rattle snake, in pure horror of his
detestable rattles, and poisonous tooth. Nay some
of them even contaminate the pure Cockney blood
of Englishmen, of which the old giants were so
excessively fond,* by mixing it with that of the
" guessing, gouging, bundling damsels" of this
detestable democracy. Not content with flirt-
ing with them, they actually marry them, that
is, when they are very rich, which indeed is some
extenuation. But in justice to these unfortunate
men, I must acknowledge that such are the pains
taken by these republican damsels to attract and
entrap our countrymen, that it is a miracle that
any one escapes. I happened to go into a shop,
not long since, to buy a laced cap, on speculation,
for which the man asked nearly twice as much as
when I looked at it some time before. On my com-
plaining of this, he replied—

" O, sir, the price of laced caps has risen a hundred per cent. lately."

" From what cause ?" said I.

" Why, sir, the truth is, that Major Tight
body the tall, handsome Englishman, has lately
arrived, and the young ladies have been pull-
ing caps for him at such a rate, that it is comput-
ed upwards of five hundred have been more or
less torn to pieces in consequence. Judging from

---

* " Fee, faw, fum,
  I smell the blood of Englishmen,
  Dead or alive I will have some."
              Jack and his bean-stalk.

13

your appearance, sir," continued he, bowing, "I
should not be surprised if you had been accessary
to the destruction of a few." Whereupon I bought
his cap without further hesitation. But to return :

The pertinacity with which these poor deluded
emigrants, persist in remaining in this miserable,
degraded, debauched, deistical country, convinces
me that people may actually be persuaded out of
their five senses. This is the only way of explain-
ing the phenomenon ; for it is impossible, by any
other hypothesis to account for their continuing
to suffer in this dog's misery when they can be
sent home free of expense, provided they will
only make affidavit on their arrival that there
is neither food, raiment, religion, law, or ho-
nesty among these republicans. As an illustration of this unaccountable attachment to misery, I will state an incident that occurred to me
in Philadelphia. In strolling about one morning,
who should I meet but the unfortunate, deluded,
and seduced emigrant I had picked out of the gutter in New-York, and procured a free passage to
England. The fellow was, as usual, pretty handsomely "corned," as my friend, the communicative traveller, has it.—On expressing my surprise,
at his being still here, in this miserable country,
he hickupped out—

"Why, please your honour, I considered better
of it afterwards"—for, says I, " this is a d——d
miserable country to be sure, but then Old England is rather worse, and a prudent man, will al-

ways stick to the lesser evil, my hearty." "Go to the ——," said I. "I'm going to the tavern," quoth he, and staggered over to the sign of some famous Yankee general; I believe they call him Washington.

CHAP. XIII.

I FOUND myself alone in the stage this morning
greatly to my satisfaction.   Nothing, indeed, is so
annoying to a well-bred Englishman, as being in
company with half a dozen of these immaculate
republicans, who think, because they pay the same
fare, they have a right to talk with any of their
fellow-passengers without ceremony.   They have,
in truth, a most detestable sociability about them,
which obtrudes itself upon every body, and pays
no more respect to a stranger in a fashionable coat,
than to an old acquaintance in rags.   They stand

as erect in the presence of a great man as in that
of a little one, and I verily believe if the king were
to come among them, they would use no more ceremony in asking him questions, than if he were a
pig-stealing judge. This insolent familiarity is
another of the precious products of the turbulent
spirit of democracy, which, by inculcating the absurd doctrine of equality, destroys that salutary
deference to wealth and splendour, without which
it is scarcely worth a man's while to be either rich
or splendid. It sickens me to see a fellow in a
thread-bare coat, and tattered wool hat, making
up to a gentleman with his head erect, and his hat
on the top of it, and asking him a question without
the least stammering or hesitation, as you will see
them do every day in this bear-garden of democracy. The pleasure I felt in being alone, was,
notwithstanding, somewhat alloyed by the idea of
travelling unarmed in this region of banditti, and
without any companions to assist me in case of an
attack. But again, when I came to recollect that
considerably more than three-fourths of the people of this puissant republic were themselves rogues
and banditti, I comforted myself with the assurance that if I had any fellow-passengers, it would
be at least three to one in favour of their robbing
me themselves, rather than protecting me from
others.

I soon found, however, that I was reckoning
without my host, in supposing I should be rid of
the annoyance of talking. The driver turned out

a most sociable fellow, and seemed to think it in-
cumbent upon him to entertain his solitary passenger.   He took occasion to inform me that one of
the houses we passed belonged to no less a person
than himself; that he was sole proprietor of one
hundred acres of land, and that he was only driving
the stage on this occasion in consequence of an
accident that happened to the person who usually
officiated.   I thought it best to humour the fellow,
having been assured by an intimate friend, (one
of the writers of the Quarterly,) that if the stage-
drivers of this country got displeased with their
passengers, they always took the first opportunity
in passing a bad piece of road, to upset the carriage and break some of their bones.   As to the risk
they themselves run on these occasions, they think
nothing of it, being at all times perfectly willing
to risk their own necks for the pleasure of re-
venging an affront.   For this reason all travellers
in this country who wish to escape with whole
bones, make a point of being agreeable to the stage-
drivers, and treating them to whiskey at every
tavern.   This is the only way they can travel with
any remote chance of safety.

    This being the case, I was resolved to humour
the fellow, and be affable; so I asked what the
accident was which procured me the honour of being driven by a republican landholder.

    " O, a mere trifle," replied he—" he happened
to get both eyes gouged out yesterday in a frolic."

" Frolic!" said I—" do they frolic here on Sundays?"

" To be sure they do—it's an idle day, and what else should they do—you wouldn't have them work would you?"

" Why no—but then they might go to church, you know."

" Church!—what's that?—O, now I recollect— I saw a church once in Nova-Scotia, but we've none in the States, so it would be rather a long Sabbath-day's journey to find one."

" Well, but they might stay at home and read the bible, or some other good book—or they might at least say their prayers."

" Read!" quoth Jehu—" why d——n me if I don't believe you're one of our bloody aristocrats! No—no—we love liberty too well to oblige our children to go to school, and they love it too well to go if we sent them. Nobody can read here but your emigrant foreigners, and that's the reason we don't allow them to vote or hold offices."

A precious admission thought I, the Quarterly shall know this. "But what becomes of your children while they are growing up, and before they are put to a trade, or can work in the fields?"

" O, they are left pretty much to themselves, to learn the habits of freemen. They play in the road, and amuse themselves with frightening horses as they come by. Or they worry the puppies and kittens for amusement, when there are no lit-

tle *niggers* to set the dogs at.   Their principle
business, however, is to learn to chew tobacco,
spit against the wind, drink whiskey, and beat
their mothers for a frolic."

A hopeful bringing up, thought I. "But is it possible that you have neither churches, preachers,
schoolmasters, nor bibles among you?"

"Not a son of a b——h of them," replied he.
"We want nothing here, and, of course, there is
no necessity for praying—nor for parsons and
churches—for your schoolmasters, they only serve
to break down the spirit of liberty, by whipping
the boys—and for the book you mention, I think
I did see one once somewhere or other, but I believe it was in Nova-Scotia."

"But what do you do then on Sundays?"

"O, we don't want for amusement—we spend
it in drinking, dirking, gouging, pig-stealing,
swearing, guessing, bundling, and other pleasant
recreations * But we begin to be tired of these,
as you know people will after a while, and besides,
there are hardly any peepers left in the whole country, and the sport of gouging begins to fail.   My
driver and myself were the only two left in forty
miles round, with a pair of eyes a piece, and he
lost both his yesterday, as I told you.   I expect
mine will go next."

"This is quite melancholy," said I.   "What
will you do when there are no eyes to be gouged

* Vide No. 58, Eng ed

out? You will have to set down like another Alex-
ander, and weep that there are no more worlds to
conquer."

"No danger of that," replied Jehu. "There
is always plenty for variety. When the eyes are all
out we fall to biting noses,* and by the time they
are getting scarce, the little boys will grow big
enough to have their eyes put out." It is like the
spring, when one flower pops up, as another fades
—when strawberries are succeeded by cherries,
and cherries by blackberries, and blackberries by
apples, pears, peaches, pumpkins, and potatoes.
But yonder is Princeton, and huzza for a dashing
drive up."

So saying he cracked his whip, put his horses to
their speed, routed a flock of sheep, ran over a lit-
ter of pigs, two blind men, and a professor of mi-
neralogy, with his pockets full of specimens, and
finished by upsetting the stage against a pump, to
the great delight of a mob of ragged little republicans, at the inn-door, who, I afterwards learned,
were students of the college pursuing their studies.
Luckily I escaped with only a broken shin, which
fortunate circumstance the rascal insisted gave him
a legitimate claim to a double allowance of whiskey
at my hands.

Princeton is the capital of old *Kentuck*, as these
republican slang-whangers call it, by way of expressing their affection for that dirking, gouging,

* Vide Quarterly, No. 58, Eng. ed.

swearing, drinking, blaspheming state.* Its principal boast is a college, in which reading and writing has lately been introduced by the Lancaster
method. There was a formidable opposition to
the introduction of these aristocratic branches of
education, but at length the parents of the students
consented on condition that the matter should stop
here. The legislature accordingly passed a law,
declaring a forfeiture of the charter in case of the
introduction of any more of these pestilent novel-
ties. The only books they are permitted to read,
are Tom Paine's works; and such is the rigour
with which this statute is enforced, that a student
was expelled the very day before my arrival, for
only having a bible in his possession. It was in
vain that he proved himself incapable of reading,
having got only as far as " No man may put off the
law"—he was made an example for the benefit of
republicanism. What became of the offending bible, cannot be certainly said, but it was whispered
that the professor of divinity, (a sort of sinecure
here) exchanged it with a pious old lady, for a
starched band which belonged to her deceased hus-
band.

Having an hour's leisure on my hands, I visited
the outside of the college, which is a log-hut of
about a hundred feet in length, with a thatched
roof, the windows of which are all broken, it being
the principal recreation of the students to try their

* Vide Quarterly.

skill, by throwing stones at a particular pane, and whoever hits it first is entitled to be head of his class for the day. I did not enter this classic fane, having been told that the penalty of such intrusion, on the part of a stranger, is a gallon of whiskey, which I did not think worth incurring. Somebody pointed out to me the field, where, as these ever-lying, ever-boasting republicans say, General Washington beat the English and Hessians most terribly, and took nine hundred prisoners.— Here I met an old British soldier, who assured me that he was not only at this, but all the battles during the American rebellion, and that so far from this being the fact, it was the British that beat General Washington, and took nine hundred prisoners of the Yankees. He further assured me that they never gained a single victory, in both their wars with England, and that their whole history was a tissue of lies from beginning to end. I asked him why he did not go to England, and write a history to that effect. " It will be reviewed in the Quarterly, which will swear to all you say ; certify that you are an honest man, and tell the truth"*—and finally praise your work, so that you will certainly make your fortune by the sale, and perhaps get a pension to boot."

" But to tell you the truth, master, I left his majesty's service without taking leave. They might—you understand ?" " By no means," said I ; " hundreds of deserters have been received and

* Vide No. 58, art. Faux.

cherished, only by telling the truth of these bragging Yankees!"

At dinner I was very much annoyed by young students, who gathered round and amused themselves
with snatching things from the table, so that in a little time there was nothing left for me to eat. At first
I had thoughts of resenting this impertinent out-
rage, but observing that each one carried a dirk,
in a side pocket, the handle of which was perfectly visible, I thought it prudent to say nothing, and
join in the laugh which accompanied every successful transfer of meat or vegetables. As it happened, however, I was sufficiently revenged, for
in the end they fell out about a favourite bit, drew
their dirks, and in less than five minutes, every
soul of them lay dead upon the floor. The uproar
brought in the landlord, two or three professors,
and a justice of the peace, who, instead of interfer-
ing stood by enjoying the frolic, as they called it,
and laughing at every successful push.

The stage now drove up, greatly to my satisfaction, as I was heartily sick of this classic abode.
Such indeed was my haste, that I jumped in without paying my bill, which the landlord politely
reminded me of. On making an apology, he replied carelessly, " O, never mind, sir, this happens so often with our republican travellers, that
I think myself well off, if one in ten pays me, and
him I always charge for all the rest." By this time
there was a crowd of ragged students gathered
about, and on its being whispered that I was cer-

tainly an Englishman, because I paid my bill, there
was a cry of " Gouge him ! gouge him !" which
certainly could have been done, had not the driver
charitably whipped up his horses, and distanced
the barbarians, who followed us for half a mile,
shouting and hallooing like Indians.

That the spirit of democracy should thus pene-
trate into the hallowed recesses of learning and
science, is not to be wondered at.   Liberty is the
root of all evil ; since nothing is more certain than
that if men have not the power to do a thing, the
will signifies nothing.   From hence it arises, that
rogues and ruffians are chained to prevent the in-
dulgence of their bad passions.   Nothing is so ef-
fectual in preventing evil, as taking away the
power of doing evil.   The more free a people are,
according to the Quarterly,* the more wicked they
will be, because the privilege of doing every thing
not forbidden by the laws, will be followed in the
natural course of things, by the liberty of doing
every thing contrary to the laws.   These axioms
are so self-evident that it is unnecessary to insist
upon them any further.

After passing through Natchitoches, Passamaquoddy, Michilimackinac, and other places, whose
appearance is as barbarous as their names, we arrived at Philadelphia, the capital of the state of
Moyamensing.   As this is considered the most
orderly, polite, civilized, and literary city of the

* Vide No. 58, Eng. ed.

14

states, I comforted myself with the hope of meeting with a different reception from what I had
been hitherto accustomed to, among these immaculate republicans, as the Quarterly says. But,
alas! my hopes rested on a foundation of sand. We
had scarcely entered the city when the stage was
stopped by a crowd of people gathered around a
dead body, that had just been killed. The history
of this transaction is as follows, and furnishes a
happy illustration of the blessings of pure democracy.

It seems a fellow named Ramsbottom, a man-
milliner by trade, and a genuine republican, had
taken offence at a neighbour whose name was
Higginbottom, because his wife had attempted to
cheapen a crimped tucker at his shop, and afterwards reported that he sold things dearer than his
rival man-milliner, over the way, whose name was
Winterbottom, and whose next door neighbour
was one Oddy. In the pure spirit of democracy,
Ramsbottom determined to dirk not only Higginbottom, but Winterbottom, and Oddy, together
with their wives, and all the Higginbottoms,
Winterbottoms, Oddys, and little Oddities. It
was a long time before he could get them all together, so as to make one job of it. At length,
he collected them all at his own house, to keep
their Christmas eve, and determined to execute
his diabolical purpose. It appears, however, that
he had changed his mind as to dirking, from what
followed, for just as they were up to their eyes in

a Christmas pye, a sudden explosion took place, the house blew up, and every soul perished, Ramsbottom, Higginbottom, Winterbottom, Oddy, the little Ramsbottoms, Higginbottoms, Winterbottoms, Oddys, and Oddities. Such is the ferocity and thirst of vengeance generated in the hot-bed of democracy, that this desperado, Ramsbottom, scrupled not like the republican Samson of old, to pull down destruction on himself, only for the pleasure of being revenged on his enemies.*

* It will be perceived that our author is very fond of this story.

Am Ed.

CHAP. XIV.

THE city of Philadelphia, (every thing is a city here) is a little higgledy-piggledy place, with hardly a decent house in it, and whose principal trade consists in the exportation of Toughy and Peppe Pot. It is ituate between two rivers, the Delaware on the West, and the Schuylkill on the East; the former is a decent sort of a river, but nothing to be compared to the Thames, or the

Avon. The streets, for the most part, are laid out in the shape of a ram's horn, at the little end of which commonly reside that class of people who have been unfortunate in business. Hence the phrase of " coming out at the little end of the horn." There are no public buildings, nor indeed any thing else worthy of a stranger's notice, and so I pass them by as unworthy of notice.

I took lodgings (for I hate your first rate hotels) at the sign of the Goose and Gridiron, where for the first time since my arrival in the states, I tasted sweet bread.* I was at a loss to account for this phenomenon, until I found my landlady was an English woman. It is a singular fact, noticed by all travellers in this country, that go where you will, the bread is sure to be sour. Whether this is owing to the yeast, to the bad taste of these republicans, or to some intrinsic quality in the wheat, I cannot say. I am rather inclined to the latter opinion, because the grapes in this country, as well as the apples, peaches, and every species of fruit I tasted, are as sour as vinegar. There must be some acidity in the soil or air, or both, to produce this disagreeable singularity. Or perhaps it is owing to the turbulent spirit of democracy after all.

It is not without some reason that Philadelphia is called the Athens of America, since, among other advances in civilization, the people sometimes

* Vide No. 58, Eng. ed.

14*

wash their hands and faces. This practice was
introduced about seven years ago, by the marquess
of Tweedale and his suite. It was at first violent-
ly opposed as an aristocratic custom, unworthy of
freemen; but it gradually made its way, and there
are now few, except the radicals and ultra democrats that demur to the practice. The popular
opinion is, however, rather against it, and it is
seldom that a person with clean hands and face is
elected to any office, unless he can demonstrate
his republicanism by a red nose, a black eye, or
some other unequivocal mark of his high calling.

The city has also a nightly watch, a peculiarity
I did not observe either at Boston or New-York.
Here watchmen are obliged to call the hour through
the whole night, an excellent regulation, as I supposed, since this is pretty good evidence of a man
being awake. But the spirit of democracy evades
every salutary regulation it seems, and I was assured by a worthy alderman, a native of England,
that these fellows from long habit, call the hour as
regularly sleeping as waking, so that this afforded
no additional security to the citizens. The alderman told me that not less than three or four watchmen were robbed at their posts every night; and
nothing was more common than a fellow to be
bawling out "all's well," when somebody was
actually picking his pockets. The alderman related a humorous instance.

It seems a sturdy watchman, who being considered the best of the gang at a nap, was always placed

at some responsible post, was in his box nodding,
when a wag of a thief took off his cap, and put in
its place a night-cap, which he had stolen from an
old apple woman who lived near the ferry stairs
in High-street, and to whose house he carried and
left the watchman's hat.　The old dame upon dis
covering the theft, set out bright and early, with
the watchman's cap on her head for want of a better, to lay her complaint before the police, when
as luck would have it, she saw the vigilant child
of the night, still nodding in his box with her cap
on his head.　The Amazon seized her property, and
cried out "stop thief" with such astonishing
vigour, that she actually awoke the watchman,
although people who best knew him thought it
was impossible.　The watchman, rubbing his
eyes, and seeing the apple woman with his cap on
her head, naturally concluded that the cry of
"stop thief" applied to her.　Upon which he carried her forthwith to the police, to which the lady
followed with great alacrity, supposing she had
the watchman in custody.　When arrived at the
police, there was the deuce to pay.　The watchman charged the apple woman with stealing his
hat, and the apple woman charged the watchman
with stealing her cap—the police officer scratched
his head, and the clerk gnawed two goose quills
to the stump.　But what was most to be admired,
two lawyers were entirely puzzled to death to de-
cide between the two; and to puzzle a Philadel-

phia lawyer, is proverbially difficult.   In conclusion, the watchman was broke, as the safest
course; but the sovereign people considering him
as an oppressed citizen, immediately elected him
an alderman.

There is a great show, or rather affectation of
literature here, and the good people crow in their
cups a good deal, on account of the oldest period-
ical paper in the states being published here.   It
is called the Port-Folio, and is really so old that it
may be justly pronounced quite superannuated. But
I did not find any other special indications of a
flourishing state of literature.   To be sure, here
and there you meet with a young lady that can
read large print, and a young gentleman that can
tell a B from a bull's foot, by the aid of a quizzing glass.   But there never has been an original
work produced here of American manufacture ;
and the only translation I ever met with, is that
of the almanac into High Dutch.   They likewise
boast of one Franklin, a great hand at flying kites,
and one of the first manufacturers of lightning rods.
I had heard him spoken of respectfully at home,
so am willing to allow he was clever.   But after
all, what have these people to boast of on this head?
Both Washington and Franklin, and indeed all
the respectable sort of men, who figure in the
history of this country, were born under the king's
government, and are therefore to all intents and
purposes Englishmen.   Franklin spent a long

time in England, and though there is no account
of Washington ever having been there, his being
able to read and write, of which there are pretty
clear proofs, is a sufficient presumption that he
must have been there, or where could he have got
his learning? At all events, they lived the best
part of their lives under the genial and fostering
influence of monarchial institutions, and that all
their talents and virtues originated in that circumstance, is proved, first, by their never having done
any thing worthy of admiration, after the establishment of the republican system here; and se-
condly, by the singular fact that from that time
to the present, there has not been a man of ordinary
talents or acquirements produced in the country.
Mr. Cooper and Mr. Irving, have, it is true, gained
some little reputation; but I am credibly informed
that the former of these gentlemen, has been once
or twice in England, and that the latter never
wrote English, until he had been long enough
there to forget the jargon of his own country So,
after all, they furnish no exemption to my rule,
which I have the happiness to say is sanctioned by
the Quarterly. As to Mr. Walsh, who had the
hardihood to tilt with the Quarterly, he I know
was a good while in England, and there it was,
beyond doubt, he polished his lance, and learned
all the arts of literary warfare. But to put the
matter at rest for ever, it is utterly impossible,
as I have sufficiently proved, for any thing elegant,
or good, or beautiful, or great, to take root in the

polluted sink of that earthly pandemonium, a genuine republic.*

Religion, like literature, is at a low ebb here,
or rather there is neither ebb nor flood, on account
of there being no religion at all. This might be
expected from the absence of an established church,
with exclusive privileges over all other denomina-
tions of sectarians. The quakers are numerous
here, and it is utterly impossible there should be
any pure orthodox religion where they predomi-
nate, since we all know that they preach volunta-
rily, as the spirit moves them, and without fee or
reward. Now, I have already proved, that a religion which costs nothing, is good for nothing.
It unquestionably is with religion as with every
thing else, the more we pay for it, the higher value
we set upon the purchase, and the better we are
likely to become.† On the contrary, a people who
get their piety gratis, must, of necessity, in a little
time, become impious. In proof of this, I was
told by my landlady, a very respectable widow,
that there was a society in each of the wards of the
city, composed of the principal quakers and others,
to put down religion altogether, by the simple and
certain means of not persecuting any particular
sect, or giving any one exclusive privileges. This
wicked design, aided by the destruction of all the
bibles which they have bought up and burnt, is
likely, my landlady assured me, to banish, at no

* Vide No. 58, Eng. ed.   † Ditto

distant period, every trace of orthodoxy from this crooked, quakerish, and abandoned city. It is better to be a bigot without religion, than religious without bigotry. Nothing, in short, leads so inevitably to an indifference to all religion, as the doctrine of toleration, which makes them all equal in the participation of wealth and civil rights. The enjoyment of superior privileges and immunities on one hand, and the deprivation of them on the other, generates a salutary opposition between the two parties, exceedingly favourable to the interests of religion. The party in the enjoyment of these superior immunities will endeavour, by superior piety, to prove that it deserves them ; and the party out of possession, will strive, by the same means, to prove that though it may not possess, it at least deserves a full share. Thus will the worst passions of the mind, envy, hatred, and fear, as it were by miracle, harmoniously conduce to the preservation and increase of the true faith. But there is nothing of this in the pure system of democracy, and consequently there is no religion but unbelief, no morals but what consists in a total relaxation of morality, and no deity but Satan, the first republican on record, as the Quarterly says.

As these immaculate republicans have neither religion nor morals, so are they entirely destitute of gratitude. It will hardly be believed, but is nevertheless a fact, that Mr. Jefferson, the author of their famous declaration of independence, the oracle of republicans, the former president of the

United States, and after Satan, the prince of democrats, the man whom the people toast at all their
public meetings, and pretend to revere next to
Washington, is, at this moment, an actor on the
Philadelphia boards for bread!* I saw him myself,
or I would not have believed it, bad as I think
these miserable republicans.   Yet, with this damn-
ing fact staring them full in the face, they are every day boasting of their gratitude to their benefac-
tors, at the gorgeous feasts given to General La
Fayette. I hope the Quarterly will touch them up
on this score in the next number Of their other
surviving presidents, Mr. Madison, as I was assured, teaches a school in some remote part of Virginia, and Mr. Adams lives in great obscurity somewhere in the neighbourhood of Boston! This is a
natural consequence of abolishing the excellent system of pensions and sinecures. I confess, I felt a
little ill-natured satisfaction, at the fate of Jefferson
and Madison, when I considered that the first
picked a quarrel with England on pretence of
maintaining the rights of his country, and the
other had the wickedness to declare war against
her, while she was struggling for the liberties of
Europe, now so happily secured in the keeping
of the Holy Alliance. Nor indeed could I find in
my heart to be sorry for Mr. Adams, who was
one of the prime movers of the rebellion, and a

---

* The author has confounded our old favourite the comedian,
with Thomas Jefferson, the late president. But this is a mistake
pardonable in a stranger.—*Am. pub.*

principal pillar of the revolution. Nothing can furnish a clearer proof of the divine right of kings,
than the fact, that history does not record an instance of a man who took arms against his sovereign, on whom some signal punishment did not
fall, by special interposition of providence.*

These reflections, which crossed my mind on
seeing an ex-president performing the character
of Diggory, were suddenly interrupted, by what
seemed the sound of a trumpet, directly behind
me. On turning round, to see what it was, I was
struck with horror—it was the little Frenchman,
blowing his nose, with his confounded flowered
Madras handkerchief. The story of the diabolical dance at Communipaw; the little black gentleman who could be no other than Satan himself,
so like the little Frenchman—all rushed upon my
mind. I grew desperate—started up—tumbled
over the people in the box—burst open the door,
and marched through the lobby into the street,
without once looking behind me. Just as I left
the box, I heard the little Frenchman say in reply
to some question, "Monsieur is not mad—diable!
he is only a little afraid of robbers."

As I walked hastily on towards my lodgings, I
heard a footstep, pat, pat, close behind me. 'Tis
the little Frenchman, thought I—and mended my
pace. Still the footsteps continued pat, pat, pat.
I began to run—still the pat, pat, pat, continued,

* Vide Quarterly Review—Clarendon's Hist. Rebellion, &c. &c.
15

until I arrived at the door of my lodgings, where necessarily stopping for a moment, till the door was opened, I felt two great paws pressing heavily upon my shoulders. The door opened, and I rushed in, almost oversetting my good landlady, who eagerly inquired what was the matter. "Satan is at my heels," replied I. "Lack-a-daisy! is that all? nobody minds him here. Indeed he is so popular that the people would send him to congress, I dare say, if he liked." "O Sodom and Gomorrah!" said I—"is there no brimstone left for these impious, rebellious, republican cities!" The worthy lady paid no attention to this apostrophe, but began to pat a great Newfoundland dog, a mighty favourite, exclaiming, "why poor old Neptune, where have you been all this while?" Then turning to me, "he must have followed you to the play-house. I noticed he took a great liking to you from the first."

The night was spent in almost sleepless anxiety. My thoughts continually reverted to the little Frenchman, the dancing gentleman at Communipaw, and the great black Newfoundland dog, until they became so connected together that I could not separate them. I became feverish with indescribable terrors; and if I chanced to fall into a doze, was ever and anon disturbed by attempts to break open my door, accompanied by strange and unaccountable moanings and whinings, for which I could not account. The spirit of democracy seemed to be letting slip all his legions of malignant fiends to torture me, and I resolved to quit for ever this city of horrors.   Accordingly I rose early, hastened my breakfast, inquired of the good landlady if there was any conveyance to the South that day.

"There is a steam-boat, which starts about this hour; but you're not going away in such a hurry?"

"This moment"—I replied, seizing my portmanteau.

"But you had better send for a porter to carry your baggage."

"Send for the d——l, in the shape of a little Frenchman, or a great black dog," said I impatiently, removing my portmanteau.

"Better call a hack then," replied she, exclaiming "'tis a long way."

"I'll not wait a minute for all the carriages in this diabolical city."

"Why then sir—you had better settle your bill before you go—if you are not in too great a hurry."

This being done, I sallied out with hasty steps towards the river, where I jumped into the first steam-boat I met with, and was felicitating myself on my escape, when I actually ran my nose right into the mahogany face of the little Frenchman. Starting back, I fell over a basket of onions belonging to an old woman, who let fly at me in the republican style.   I was now satisfied in my own mind—"He must be either the evil one, or he deals with the evil one. and is therefore a witch." To ease myself of these distracting doubts, after we had left the wharf, I called the captain of the steam-boat aside, related my story, and proposed tying the Frenchman neck and heels, and throwing him overboard, to see if he would sink or swim. The brute, who I have no doubt was also in league with Satan, laughed in my face and replied—

"I would oblige you with pleasure, but we are not allowed to try witches nowadays, in this manner."

"Not try witches!" cried I in astonishment—"what d'y'e do with them then?" Another proof thought I, of the absence of all law as well as gospel here.

"Why we generally let them run—the old boy will get them at last you know, and pay them for all their pranks. But, to tell you truth, we don't believe much in witches nowadays."

"Nor in fairies?"

"No."

"Nor in the Prince of Hohenlohe's miracles?"

"No, I never heard of him."

"Nor Johanna Southcote's?"

"No, I never heard of her either?"

"Nor Vampyres?"

"No."

"Nor ghosts?"

"Not a single mother's son of them."

"And what do you suppose has become of them all?"

" They went away about the time the race of
giants and mammoths disappeared, I suppose."

" In the name of heaven," cried I, to this unbelieving reprobate—"what do you believe then?"

" Why I believe the moon is not made of green
cheese, and that the little Frenchman is no witch,"
quoth he, and went coolly about his business.

He had just gone from me when the little
Frenchman came up, and offered his box.

" Ah monsieur—you ran away from me last
night, but I have caught you again this morning—
diable—I believe the fates ordain we shall never
part again." Heaven forbid, thought I, but remained silent, hardly knowing what to say

" Is monsieur going to New Orleans yet?" continued he after a short pause.

" I am on my way," replied I, with as much
the air of distant hauteur as I could muster up on
the occasion.

" Then monsieur has somehow or other turned
his nose the wrong way again. Diable! you are
going back to Portsmouth, as sure as a pistol."

Thou father of lies and deceit, thought I, you
shall not impose upon me again, either in the
shape of a little Frenchman, or a great black dog.
So I said nothing, but eyed him with a look of
most mortifying incredulity. He shrugged up his
shoulders, took a pinch of snuff, and walked away,
to frisk among the ladies, with whom the old
Harry has always been somewhat a favourite. The

15*

captain, who had just been ashore to steal a score
or two of pigs, for the supply of his passengers,
soon after came up, and asked me with a smile if
I had found out whether the little man was a witch
or not? I evaded his question, in the true republican style, by asking which way we were going,
south or north.

"Why north, to be sure, sir."

"Towards New-Orleans?"

"No--right from it as straight as an arrow."

"And why didn't you tell me so?" replied I
in a rage, for I could not stand this imposition.

"I did, as soon as you inquired. "It's not
my business to tell every passenger the way to
New-Orleans. Every steam-boat is not going
there, and the best thing a stranger can do is to
ask before he goes on board."

I now positively insisted that he should turn the
vessel right about, and land me where he took me
up.

"What, go back twenty-miles, with a hundred
people, to rectify the blunder of one! No—no—
sir, you must go on to Bristol. I shall return in
the morning, and take you back, so you will only
lose one day after all. But here comes the witch,
perhaps he will take you back on a broomstick"—-
So saying he went away without paying any attention to my remonstrances. Presently the little
Frenchman came up, and inquired what was the
matter. I stated my case, and asked his advice,

for at this moment I felt that to trust to Satan himself was better than to rely on a republican.

"What shall I do?" said I.

"Appeal to posterity and the immortal gods!" said he, with an air of diabolical sublimity, at the same time taking a mortal pinch of snuff that smelt like brimstone.

"There are no gods in this impious country," answered I in despair—" and as for posterity, I am a bachelor and never mean to be married—so I can have no posterity!"

"There is a way, Monsieur," quoth the little Frenchman with an insinuating diabolical smile.

"What!" cried I, with an ungovernable burst of indignation—" would you tempt me, Satan! But thy arts are vain.   No, diabolical instigator. Know I am a true-born Englishman, a defender of the faith and a bulwark of religion.   No! be thou Asmodeus, Ashtaroth, Belshazzar, or the Devil on two Sticks—be all mankind extinct, for want of posterity, and be there no posterity to appeal to, let me be going north or south, or east or west, to New-Orleans or New-Guinea, all this shall happen before Satan shall tempt me to the sin of—."

"Of what?" said the little d——l of a man.— "Of what shall never defile my tongue in the utterance," said I, with the air of a hero.

"Well, if Monsieur will neither appeal to posterity, nor to the immortal gods, there is no more to be said.   And now I think of it, no more is necessary.   See! we are just at Bristol, where they land passengers. You can stop here to-night, and return to Philadelphia to-morrow morning. I am sorry to lose your agreeable company, but I am going on a little way farther to the north."

This last information was of itself sufficient to determine me to take his advice, though I could not help suspecting in my own mind that he had some diabolical design in his head. Accordingly here I landed, the little Frenchman taking leave of me in the most friendly manner. " I am sorry, to lose Monsieur's agreeable company—but as I am going north, and Monsieur south, who knows but we may meet again?" Heaven forbid, thought I, as they loosed the rope, and the boat ploughed her way down the stream.

I found out a lodging where I ordered supper, and while it was getting ready, could not help reflecting on the brutal inhospitality, the unfeeling rudeness and ferocity generated in the polluted hot-bed of republicanism. The conduct of the Captain of the steam-boat, in first receiving me on board—his refusal to turn back only twenty or thirty miles to land me again—and the brutal indifference with which the passengers listened to my just complaints —all these rushed together on my mind, and put me into such a passion that I determined to be revenged on the whole race of republicans, by going to bed without my supper, which I did to the utter discomfiture of the landlord, the chambermaid, the ostler, and particularly the cook, who killed himself with a spit, in a fit of despair, at my refusing to taste his terrapin soup.

CHAP. XV.

Good luck of the author in not being robbed—Story of the roaring republican Ramsbottom—Steam-boat—Fat lady of colour —Force of bad example—Spirit of democracy—Privilege of speech, a lias impudent loquacity—Author beleaguered by a wandering republican gentleman, who tells his story—Author's reflections on it—Insolent republican custom of shaking hands —Goes to a magistrate—Another sketch of a republican justice—Republican mode of settling law-suits—Takes French leave of his worship.

Luckily, though alone and unarmed, having lost my pistols as before stated, I escaped being murdered that night, which good fortune I attribute to the attention of the people having been called off by an affair which took place during the evening. I shall relate it, for the purpose of illustrating the true spirit of democracy.

It seems a fellow by the name of Ramsbottom, a man-milliner by trade, and a great stickler for the rights of man, had taken offence at a neighbour whose name was Higginbottom, because his wife had attempted to cheapen a crimped tucker at his

shop, and afterwards reported all over town that
he, Ramsbottom, sold his things much dearer than
his rival man-milliner over the way, whose name
was Winterbottom, and whose next door neighbour
was one Oddy.   In the pure spirit of democracy,
Ramsbottom determined to dirk not only Higginbottom, Winterbottom, and Oddy, together with
their wives, but likewise all the little Higginbottoms, Winterbottoms, Oddys, and little Oddities.
It was several years before Ramsbottom could get
the whole party together, so as to make one job of
it.   At last, after an interval of about ten years,
he collected them all at his house, to keep their
Christmas-eve, and determined then and there to
execute his diabolical purpose.   It would appear,
however, that he had previously changed his mind
as to the dirking, probably on account of the trouble of killing so many, one after the other, for just
as they were all up to the eyes in a Christmas pie,
made of four-and-twenty blackbirds, an explosion
took place—the house blew up, and every soul,
Ramsbottom, Higginbottom, Winterbottom, Oddy, their wives, together with all the young Ramsbottoms, Higginbottoms, Winterbottoms, Oddys,
and Oddities, were scattered in such invisible
atoms, that not a vestige of them was ever afterwards discovered.   Such is the deadly spirit of re-
vengeful ferocity, generated in the polluted sink of
democracy.   The desperado, Ramsbottom, who
was considered rather a peaceable person, among
these barbarians, scrupled not, like the old repub-

lican Samson, to pull down destruction on his own
head, that he might be revenged upon a poor woman for cheapening a crimped tucker.

This affair set the people talking and tippling
all night, and to this circumstance I ascribe
my good fortune in escaping being robbed and
murdered, the usual fate of strangers, whose ill-
fortune detains them at this place after dark. In
the morning the steam-boat stopped, as the little
Frenchman told me she would; and taking the
precaution to inquire whether she was going North
or South, I went on board. The Yankee Captain
saluted me with a good-humoured smile enough,
and observed, "You are going the right way now,"
but I took no notice of his insolent familiarity. At
breakfast I was seated opposite a dish of terrapin
soup, and next to a fat lady of colour, who desired
me to help her to some, which she devoured with
infinite satisfaction, although you could distinguish
the fingers and toes of the poor little terrapins, as
plain as day. I could not stand this exhibition of
cannibalism, but rushed on deck to relieve my oppressed feelings. That these white republicans,
destitute as they are of all traces of human feeling,
should indulge in this detestable dish, was not
to be wondered at ; but that the people of colour
should thus commit the unnatural crime of feed-
ing upon their own flesh and blood, was enough
to deprive them of all sympathy. But this only
shows the force of a bad example. Looking up as
they do to the whites, as their superiors in every

respect, they naturally imitate them even in their crimes, and eat terrapin soup because they see their betters do it.

During the passage up the river to Philadelphia, I was as usual annoyed by the obtrusive impertinence of the spirit of democracy. Having fought seven years for the freedom of speech, these people seem determined to enjoy the full benefit of their struggles. Morning, noon, and night, in stage-coaches and steam-boats, they will talk, whether there is any body willing to listen or not, and one reason why they never go to church, is because they would there be under the necessity of remaining quiet for at least one whole hour. Strangers in particular are sure to be specially annoyed with their forward loquacity, and it is sufficient that a man appears to be a foreigner, and to prefer solitude, to ensure his being intruded upon, by some one of these talking republicans. If you won't tell them who you yourself are, what is your business, where you came from, and whither you are going, it is all one to them ; they will turn the tables upon you, and tell you their own story.— Nay, rather than not talk, they would enter into a voluntary confession of murder, and plead guilty to a breach of the whole decalogue.*

One of the most inveterate of these talkers beleaguered me on this occasion. " I reckon you're a stranger," said he, coming up to where I was, apart from the rest, leaning over the railing as

* Vide Quarterly.

usual, pondering on the barbarity and wickedness of these immaculate republicans. I made him no answer. "You don't seem to be one of our people?" continued he inquiringly. No answer. "I guess you're an Englishman." This fellow, thought I, has some little cleverness; he has observed the superiority of my dress and air. "What makes you think so?" replied I, in a tone of distant condescension. "Why, somehow or other you English always seem to be out of sorts, as if something were on your conscience like. You go moping and moping about by yourselves, and if any body speaks to you, you look as if you would eat them up. Now we Yankees think there is no great harm in speaking to any man, in a civil way, and that a civil question is worth a civil answer any time."

I debated a moment whether I should turn my back upon him, pull out my fifty-eighth number of the Quarterly, (which I had procured in Philadelphia,) and take no further notice of this fellow. But somehow or other, I did not like his looks. He was a tall, muscular figure, straight as an arrow, with a keen, large eye, and an air of insolent independence, that seemed to challenge equality with any man, in spite of the plain simplicity of his garments. Besides, he had much the look of an expert gouger, and I thought it better to listen to his impertinence than lose my eyes.

"And so," said I at last, "you don't like us Englishmen."

16

" Why, I can't say that exactly; but if you would not take such pains to make yourselves disagreeable, we should like you a great deal better. We have had some pretty hard brushes with you to be sure, but we Yankees are a people that soon forget injuries, so long as you don't insult us. Now, for my part, I'd rather a man would cut off my head at once, than spit in my face. We don't like to be insulted."

" But who insults you?"

" Why, I don't know—but somehow or other it strikes me, that when a man comes into a strange country, the people have a right to talk to him civilly, and it is rather bad manners in him not to answer. It looks as if he thought himself better than other people. Now we Yankees fought seven years to make ourselves equal to any people on earth, and what's more, we are determined to be so, let what will happen."

" I'm sure nobody prevents you."

" Prevents us! No, I reckon that would be rather a difficult matter. But we Yankees can tell an Englishman half a mile off, by his being so shy. He seems as if he was too good to be spoken to. Now we think a man was made to be spoken to, or else there is no use in being able to speak at all."

" Nobody hinders you from talking."

" Yes—but there is such a thing as not being answered, and this, as I said, is what we don't like. If we ask you questions about yourselves or your country, it is a proof we feel some curiosity about you—and if we tell you about ourselves and our business, it is that we don't suspect you of being rogues who would take advantage of us, by knowing our business."

" But can't a man, especially in this free country, take his choice whether he shall talk or be silent?"

" To be sure he can. But then when he takes his choice whether to answer a civil question or not, he must also take his choice sometimes whether he will be knocked down or not. To refuse to answer a question—I mean a question put in a civil way, and without meaning to give offence, is to insult the man that asks it. Now what can be done with a man who will neither answer a civil question, nor resent an uncivil one by word of mouth? There is but one way, and that is to knock him down. If that don't make him speak, I don't know what will."

An excellent method. Here's your true republican ethics, thought I—but there was no use in quarrelling with the fellow, so I thought it best to humour him.

" And so you don't like us Englishmen because we don't talk?"

" That is one reason. We think a man that can't open his mouth in a strange country, except to find fault with every thing, had better stay at home, and keep himself in a good humour."

" Very well. Is that your only reason?"

" Not altogether. You go home and tell lies about us, after staying at our houses, and being treated in the best way we can.   There was last spring a year ago, a fellow that fell sick at my house of an ague and fever, and staid with me two months without paying a cent, for I scorn to take board of any man.   Would you believe it! He wrote a book when he went back to England, wherein he said my home was as dirty as a pig-pen—my wife a slut—my children savages—my-self a pig-stealer, and my country a den of drunk-ards, gougers, thieves, and men-killers.   Aye, and the worst of it was, that he made as if I had told him so myself, and so belied my countrymen. I am neither gouger, dirker, thief, nor man-killer, but"—and here his eye lightened with terrible fe-rocity—" if I ever meet that man again in this country, he or I shall have daylight shine through us."

" And so then you dislike us Englishmen be cause we won't talk to you, nor praise you?"

" We don't want you to praise us—only speak of us as we are—tell the truth, the whole truth, and nothing but the truth.   It's a dirty business to come here, and eat and drink at our tables, and sleep under our roofs—perhaps, sometimes, in the same room with our wives and children, and then go home and publish to the world that we have neither manners nor decency, because we did not send you to lay in the woods rather than receive you as it were into the very bosoms of our family. For my part I should be ashamed to look my dear country in the face, did I turn a stranger from my door, because I had no where to put him but in the same room with myself, my wife, and my children."

"Well, but," said I in a soothing tone, "you should not mind what these people say. They are a set of low, contemptible fellows, who want to get a little money, and have no other way of doing it but by telling a parcel of lies to please the vulgar."

"I know it. But still it's no way to abuse us, and then find fault with us for not liking you. Every man in the United States is a part of his country as much as a sailor is of a ship, and if you want his friendship you must not run down either."

"But to return to the subject of answering questions. You Yankees are thought to be rather too much given to that practice.

"Well," replied he, smiling and showing a set of teeth white as snow, "I believe there may be some thing in that. But the truth is, we take an interest in every thing going on in the world, and we like to hear the news. Then we frequently, in the course of our lives, change our professions three or four times, and like to collect all we can from strangers as well as others, in the way of information. What is of no use to the farmer or tradesman, may come in play when he gets to be a member of congress or a judge, and for this reason he wishes to learn as much as possible of every body he meets. Most people like to show their knowledge, so there is no offence in asking them."

I began to be tired of this tall fellow's prating,
and to get rid of the trouble of answering his questions, rather than from any curiosity, asked him
concerning a few particulars which led to the following relation.   There is no way of gaining a
genuine Yankee's heart so effectually as asking him
for the history of his life and adventures.   They
are all Robinson Crusoes in their own opinion, and
never lose an opportunity of playing the hero of a
story, even if they should invent it themselves. *

  " I was born in New-Hampshire ; raised in the
western part of the state of New-York ; married
in Ohio ; and am now settled, for the present, in
the state of Missouri."   Jupiter, thought I, the
man has travelled over half the globe in three lines.
" I have been a man of various enterprise, and
miscellaneous occupation.   At seventeen years I
commenced land surveyor in the Genesee country, which was then something of a wilderness,
and hardly afforded me employment, so that I had
sufficient leisure to visit my native town and get
married.   I forgot that neither my wife nor myself were worth ten dollars.   However, we don't
forget such things long, that's one comfort.   We
returned to Genesee with one dollar in my pocket,
and none in that of my wife.   For some time I
did not make much money ; but then we had plenty of children, which, in a new country, are better than money.   However, I managed to save a
little every year, with the intention of buying a
few hundred acres of land.   But the land rose in

* Vide Quarterly.

price faster than I made money. So that by the time I had got together five hundred dollars, land was a dollar and a half an acre. This won't do for me, thought I; but just then the people began to talk of Ohio, where land was selling at that time for two and six-pence an acre. 'Betsey,' said I, 'shall we go to Ohio?' 'To the end of the world, John,' replied she; and away we scampered the next day. Here I bought a good stout farm, cut down some trees for a place for my house, girdled others for a place for my wheat, and built a log house, twenty feet long at least. People soon flocked round, so that in a little time there was some occasion for law: so they made me a justice of the peace. Not long after, it was thought but proper to introduce a little religion: so I took to reading a sermon every Sunday, at the request of my neighbours. By-and-by, it was thought prudent to embody a company of militia for protection against the Indians; so they made me a captain of militia. In a year or two, there was a town laid out and a court-house built. This introduced two new wants—that of a judge and a town treasurer—so they made me a judge, and a town treasurer. The establishment of a town, brought with it the want of a newspaper: so a newspaper was set up, and I volunteered as editor.

" These honours were very gratifying to be sure, but all this time my family was increasing both in size and number. I had six girls and five boys, some of them six feet high. I began to be uneasy about providing for all these. I had only sixteen hundred acres of land, and that was not enough for them all. The thought struck me I could sell it for enough to buy six or eight thousand in Missouri territory. 'Betsey,' said I, 'will you go to Missouri?' 'To the end of the world, John,' said the brave girl. So the next day but one we hied away to Missouri, where I bought a few thousand acres. We were almost alone at first; but in a year or two people came faster and faster, so that from a territory we became a state, and wanted members of congress. So they made me a member of congress. But the country is getting too thickly settled for me—and I think next year of moving up the river five or six hundred miles, to get out of the crowd. I am now on my way to the Federal City, where I mean to make speeches like a brave fellow. But see, we are just arrived, and I must look to my baggage." He then shook me by the hand, and gave me a hearty invitation to come and see him next summer, when I should probably find him somewhere about the mouth of the Yellow-Stone. I thanked him, as in duty bound, and so we parted.

This wandering Gentile may stand for the whole progeny of democracy. Such is their utter indifference to home, and all its delightful associations, that rather than stay there, and get upon the parish, they will leave their kindred, friends, and household gods, to herd with Indians and buffaloe in the pathless wilderness. If they cannot live in one place, they try another—if they cannot thrive by one trade, they turn to another; and so ring the changes until they succeed at last. Hence, as a natural consequence, they turn drunkards, swearers, dirkers, spitters, bundlers, gougers, and blasphemers, caring neither for God nor man, and finally sink into the polluted pool of diabolical democracy, a prey to bitter remorse and consuming recollections.*

I am reminded by the familiarity of this backwoodsman, of the filthy republican practice of shaking hands, which prevails in this country. Such is their insolent familiarity, originating doubtless in the turbulent spirit of democracy, that the most ragged genius that labours in the streets or fields, will thrust forth his brawny paw, to shake hands with the President himself, who would be considered unworthy of his station if he declined this insolent familiarity. If two strangers happen to travel together two or three days in a stage, they cannot part without shaking hands; and this insufferable assurance extends so far, that I have been actually more than once insulted, by being offered the hand of a landlord, at whose house I happened to sojourn for a few days. On being introduced to a person, no matter how inferior, he would feel himself terribly affronted, and ten to one gouge you, if you declined his offered hand. Such is the vulgar hale-fellow-well-met familiarity engendered by the possession of equal rights, and

* Vide Quarterly.

the absence of a king and nobility to teach the people their proper distance.*

When I came to pay my fare, the Captain, with a smile of unpardonable insolence, declined receiving it, observing, that as I had gone up the river with him by mistake, he could not in conscience charge any thing for bringing me back again. I had no doubt that he did this merely to escape the consequences of having put me to the expense and inconvenience of twice travelling backwards and forwards, thirty or forty miles. But I was resolved not to let him off so easily, and accordingly the moment I landed inquired the way to a magistrate. I found this worthy seated in his office, which, judging from appearances, must have been at no distant date, a stable or a pig-sty. His worship, before I could open my business desired me to wait a little, " and be d——d to me," till he was at leisure. It seems he was receiving the report of Master Constable, who had been out on a scouting party. The following dialogue passed between them :

" Well, Simon, where are your prisoners ?"

" I caught them." It would have been too much for the spirit of equality to have added, " Your worship."

" Well, what did you do with them ?"

" I gave the defendant fifteen lashes."

" And what did you do with the plaintiff ?"

" I gave him fifteen lashes too?"

" And what did you do with the person who laid the information?"

" Why I gave him twenty-five lashes for giving us so much trouble."

" You did right," said his worship; " these rascals ought to be discouraged."

I began to commune with myself, that if this was the republican mode of administering justice, the less I had of it the better.   After hesitating a moment, whether it was worth while to receive twenty-five lashes for the pleasure of seeing the Captain get fifteen, and finding the balance rather against me, I made his worship a low bow, and departed without further ceremony. In going out I heard his worship say to Simon—" Curse that fellow ; if I was not just now engaged on a pig-stealing party, with the mayor and alderman, I'd lay him by the heels."*

* Vide Quarterly

CHAP. XVI.

Author's malediction on Philadelphia—Quarterly—Is again beleaguered by a modest republican—Their conversation—Various accidents and lucky escapes at Natchitoches, Vincennes,
Wheeling, Vandalia, Tombigbee, Big and Little Sandy—Big
and Little Muddy, and Big Dry Rivers—Arrival at Baltimore
—Insolence of the Baltimoreans—Buys a horse and sulky to
escape the intrusion of the spirit of democracy—Terrible picture of slavery—Pine woods—Stops at a lone house which
turns out to be the rendezvous of banditti—Providential escape—Leaves his watch behind—Despatches Pompey—Pompey's account of his mission to Old Hobby—Arrival at Washington.

LEAVING my malediction upon the city, the
people, the magistracy, and every living thing
else within it, I departed from Philadelphia, as
usual out of humour with the world, and disgusted with the whole clan of immaculate republicans.
As we were rapidly passing up the river towards
the south, I retired as far from every body, as I
could, and sat down to look over the fifty-eighth
number of the Quarterly, in order to refresh my
memory with some of the most striking beauties

of the turbulent spirit of democracy. But go where you will, it is impossible to keep clear of the intrusion of these free and easy republicans. While thus occupied, one of the most decently dressed and respectable republicans I had hitherto seen, came walking back and forth, passing and repassing before me. I laid down my book and went into the cabin for a moment, to get my handkerchief, which I had left there, and which I found exactly in the same place. This I mention as one of the wonders of this new world.

Returning to my post, I found this modest gentleman had taken up my book and was turning over the leaves, but he condescended to return it to me with an apology for the liberty he had taken.

" I felt some anxiety to see it," said he, "as I perceive it contains the article on Mr. Faux's Travels, which was omitted in the re-publication here."

" Indeed !" replied I with cool indifference ; " pray what was the cause of their omission ?"

" I understand it contained certain libellous passages concerning a respectable gentleman in this country, and his connexions. For my part I think it ought to have been preserved. A criticism degenerating into a string of libels, is a curiosity peculiar to the present refined age of literature."

" The greater the truth, the greater the libel,

17

said I. "Your countrymen I hope are not afraid
or ashamed of the truth."

"No, not when we can get it pure and unmix-
ed. But sketches at best degenerating into carica-
ture, and for the most part drawn from the very
worst specimens of manners, and by persons animated by the worst feelings of hostility, who have
not even the discretion to hide their malignity
are not subjects of very pleasing contemplation,
certainly."

I took up the book, and opening it at the review of Faux, began questioning the man, as follows, making it my text.

"Can you deny, sir, that it is the very nature
of a democracy to make men turbulent, ill-man-
nered, ferocious, drunken, beastly, and rude to
the last degree?"*

"I have in some measure brought this discus-
tion on my head," replied he with a smile, "and
will answer you in a different manner than I
should do under other circumstances. Cast your
eyes around the deck; there are probably seven-
ty, perhaps a hundred persons in sight. They
come in all likelihood from almost every section
of the United States, and are of different grades,
stations, occupations, and education. Do you see
any one drunk?"

I looked around, and though the deck was covered with men, women, and children, wallowing

* Vide No. 58, Eng. ed.

like swine in the filth of debauchery, replied,
" why—no—I can't say I do exactly ;" being resolved to hear what the gentleman had to say for
himself.

" Do you observe any appearance of turbulence,
rudeness, ferocity, or indecency ?"

Just then a couple of deacons set to, and gouged
out each other's eyes ; but I was resolved to see
nothing, and replied—

" None in the least."

" Do you apprehend, sir, if this drunkenness,
rudeness, turbulence, ferocity, this dirking, gouging, swearing, and impiety, were so universal a
characteristic as the Quarterly is pleased to affirm,
there would not be some examples exhibited here
among so many persons, of such various occupations and characters, coming from all parts of the
United States?"

"O, certainly, certainly," said I, with a glance
directing his attention to a fellow who had just
dirked his second cousin, and thrown him overboard.   But my gentleman kept his countenance
in a manner worthy a true disciple of brazen democracy.

" I will not pretend to deny," continued this
intolerable proser, " that our people have something of the wild flavour about them, or that they
partake in some degree of the imperfections incident to their history and situation.   Let your travellers tell us of these in the spirit of friendly ad-
monition, and show the same frankness in dis-

playing our good qualities, that they do in reprobating our faults. Accustomed as Europeans are to a world a little on the wane, they are too apt to mistake the manly frankness of freemen, for a forward impudence, and to confound the virtues of independence of spirit, with the opposite vices of a freedom from all salutary restraints. The want of that sense of inferiority, which makes the subjects of a monarch pay such abject deference to rank and wealth, is too often mistaken for rudeness ; and thus the very sense of personal independence which is essential to the preservation of freedom, is laid to our charge as a proof of barbarism and ferocity. But," continued he, smiling, " if perchance you are a traveller of the literary class, I may sometime hence figure in your book as an example of that inveterate love of talking which has been ascribed to our people. I shall therefore conclude by observing that the difference is, that our world is not quite ripe, and yours is a little decayed. We think our world is the better for blooming in all the freshness of youth ; while you appear to be of opinion that your world, like a cheese, is the better for being a little rotten." He then slightly bowed and left me, before I had time to make a cutting reply. But I was determined to pay him off at a proper time.

After passing through the towns of Natchitoches, Vincennes, Utica, Vandalia, and Tombigbee, and crossing the Big Sandy, and Little Sandy, not forgetting the Big Muddy, and Little Muddy rivers,

(did ever christian man hear such names?) we arrived at the great city of Baltimore. I should not
omit to mention that I was robbed at Natchitoches,
gouged at Utica, roasted at a log fire in Vandalia,
and dirked at Tombigbee. Besides these accidents,
I was all but drowned in Big Dry River, but luckily escaped by its having no water in it. This
was a pretty tolerable chapter of accidents for one
day, and may serve as an antidote to the delusions
of transatlantic speculation, the seductions of Mr.
Birkbeck, and the democratic slang of Miss
Wright, Capt. Hall, and the rest of the radical fry
of democracy, as the Quarterly says.*

It was my intention to spend two or three days
at Baltimore, but happening to take a walk on the
morning of my arrival, I encountered a monument
purporting to have been erected to the memory of
certain persons who fell in an action with the British in the late war, and in which the latter were
defeated, and their commander, General Ross,
killed. There was no standing this insolent exhibition of republican vanity, and I determined to stay
no longer in a place where such studied attempts
are made to mortify the feelings of Englishmen,
and perpetuate hostility between the two nations.
There is also another monument erecting here to
the memory of the rebel Washington, an additional proof of the justice with which this place has
been denounced, as the very sink of democracy.

* Vide No. 58, Eng. ed.

17*

Accordingly I bought a horse and sulky, being resolved for the future to travel by myself, in order to get rid of the impertinent intrusions of these free and easy republicans, and enjoying my own company unmolested. For this purpose I crossed over to the eastern shore of Maryland, and travelled on a by-road to the city of Washington.

I thought the negroes were bad enough off in New-England, but it was nothing to what I saw here. The road was lined with naked negroes on each side, begging for charity, this being their only refuge from absolute starvation, as their masters allow them nothing. Instead of scarecrows to frighten the birds from the corn, you generally see negroes hung up in the fields for that purpose. I cut one poor fellow down just in time to save his life, and on inquiring the cause of his being thus inhumanly punished, he told me his only offence was eating a piece of mouldy bread, which he found one day in the cupboard! Yet such is the force of habit, that this miserable wretch, instead of thanking me for saving his life, skipped over a six rail fence, joined a party of blacks at work in the field, and struck in with might and main in the songs they were singing! I thought of the fable of the swan, singing in the agonies of death, and drove on.

Towards evening, the road led through a country of thick melancholy pines, which deepened the approaching gloom, and the houses became farther and farther separated. I had now proceeded several miles without seeing a habitation, or meeting a single human being. The night was fast approaching, and I began to anticipate a lodging in the woods, when, to my great joy, I saw a light gleaming, or flickering, at fitful intervals, through the branches of the trees. As I approached, I could distinguish by the light of the moon, which now rose in cloudless majesty, a desolate, dilapidated mansion, the windows of which were for the most part broken, and the walls in half ruins. Two or three dogs saluted me as I rode up, with a republican growl, which were chid by a shrill voice, crying—" Be quiet Nap—get out Cæsar, you villain." The dogs obeyed the voice, and sneaked away.

" Who's there?" continued the same voice.

" A traveller," replied I, " who is benighted, and in want of food as well as rest. Can you accommodate me for the night?"

Here was a pause of a minute, during which the female went into the house to consult the master, as I supposed, for at the expiration of that time a man came forth, and in a hoarse voice said to me :—

" We can give you a bed and supper, such as they are. Alight sir, and my boys will see to your horse."

I accordingly entered the house through a door which opened directly into a large room, at one end of which there was a brisk fire, which served instead of candles. " Sit down," said the old man,

handing me a straw-bottomed chair, " and we will
see what we can get you for supper. Clementina!"
said he, raising his voice.

" I'm coming, daddy," answered somebody,
and forthwith in came Clementina, a damsel of at
least six feet in her stockings. She looked like a
sibyl, with eyes black as a coal, wild as those of
an antelope, and long lank hair, glossy and straight,
hanging about her neck and shoulders. I confess
I felt rather odd at seeing her, but my feelings
were nothing to those which rushed over me on
entrance of the two *boys*, as the old man called
them. They were at least seven feet high, raw-
boned and savage in their aspect, with nothing on
them but a linen shirt and trowsers. Though I
came in a fashionable gig, and was dressed in the
most fashionable travelling costume, they seemed
not to feel the least embarrassment at my presence,
but took chairs and sat down at my side with the
genuine air of republican insolence. I tried all I
could to look dignified, but in spite of myself
could not repress certain apprehensions, which
gradually came over me, and undermined my
sense of superiority. The old man and his wife,
who by the way though apparently advanced in
years, was as tall and as straight as the rest of them,
asked me a great many questions in the way of
guessing and reckoning, while Clementina bestir-
red herself in preparing and bringing in the supper.

When it was ready they all sat down without

ceremony, and with as little ceremony invited me
to follow their example.   Here was a practical illustration of the blessings of equality; but I was
determined to put up with their insolence for one
night.   The supper consisted of loads of meat,
ham, venison, game of various kinds, in quantities
sufficient to feast an army.   I began to sum up the
probable amount of my bill, as I concluded I should
have to pay for the feasting of the whole family,
and what was left besides.   "Help yourself," said
the old man, "and don't be a stranger—I'm sorry
we have nothing better—but you're heartily welcome."   Most people are welcome, thought I, for
their money, but I said nothing.

"We cannot afford tea and coffee," continued
the old man, "but here is some old whiskey that
I hope you will like.   Come, help yourself, and
here's to old Hickory."

My stomach turned at the very smell of this execrable beverage, but recollecting the republican
custom of roasting their particular friends by a
log fire for refusing to drink, I thought fit to help
myself, and make as if I drank.   In this way supper passed off smoothly enough, and the old man
then directed Clementina to make arrangements
for the night.   "You boys will be obliged to give
up your room to the stranger, and Clementina will
make you up one in the corner here."   While
this was doing, I amused, or rather perplexed myself in looking about the room, and wondering
where these people could procure such luxuries as

venison and wild game. But as the light flashed
in a remote and obscure corner on one side of the
fireplace, I was struck with horror at seeing three
rifles hanging one below the other upon hooks
fixed in the wall. The whole truth flashed upon
me at once. I am in a den of banditti, thought I,
and my moments are numbered. They will murder me to night, and none will know my wretched
fate. The old man will lay out all my money to-
morrow in whiskey—the boys will go a courting
in my new gig, dressed in my dandy coats, and
Clementina will figure in my patent corsettes. I
burst into tears at the awful anticipation.

"What ails you?" said the old man.

"May-be he has got the stomach-ach," quoth
the old hag, who now began to look just like one
of the great unknown's remarkable old women.

"Take a little more whiskey," said Clementina,
with a look of diabolical tenderness.

At first I was going to reject it with infinite contempt, but on second thoughts, and considering
what I had to go through that night, I determined
to fortify myself with Dutch courage after the
manner of the Yankees, and if I must die, die like
immortal Cæsar, with decency.

"Your bed is got ready," said Clementina, but
I determined to sit up and defer my fate as long
as possible. They now began to yawn, and one
after the other retired, wishing me good night, until decency obliged me to follow their example.
My room opened directly from that in which we

were sitting, and where the two boys were to sleep, no doubt, as I felt assured, to be handy for murdering me. I retired to my room the door of which I attempted to fasten, but there was nothing but a latch. I looked at the sheets, but they were white as snow, Clementina having, as I concluded, taken the precaution to pick out a pair that was not stained with blood, so as not to alarm me. I looked under the bed, and discovered something that greatly resembled a trapdoor, with leathern hinges.

This discovery overset me entirely. I paced my room to and fro, and listened in breathless anxiety to every sound. If a mouse stirred, my heart leapt into my throat. I heard the owl and the whippoorwill, those ill-omened birds, screeching and flapping their wings at my window, and mingling their shrill warnings with the distant howlings of half-famished wolves. I was determined not to lie down, for fear of going to sleep, and at length to while away the time, took up the fifty-eighth number of the Quarterly. But this only added to my boding apprehensions. As I read of the gougings, bundlings, dirkings, and guessings; of roasting alive on red-hot log fires—of ten dollars being the price of a man's life in this country, and of all the diabolical horrors of turbulent democracy, my spirit failed me, and I sunk insensibly on the floor.

How long I remained in this unconscious state, I cannot say, but I was roused at length by a noise of mingled howlings, barkings, cacklings, and crowings, that entered my very soul. Presently after I heard a stirring in the next room, and a light shone through my keyhole. It is all over with me now, thought I—my time is come— " Now I lay me down to sleep," said I to myself, and waited in desperate suspense. At length I ventured to look through the keyhole, where I saw a sight that froze me into horror. The two young banditti had taken down their rifles, and while loading them the following dialogue passed between them in whispers—

" D——n him but I'll do his business; I'll give him his bitters."

" Hush !" replied the other, " you'll wake the gentleman."

Again there was a confused noise of howling, barking, and cackling without. "Now is our time," said one, and both of them made, not for my door, but out of that which led into the yard. I breathed again for a moment, until I heard two guns fired at a little distance. They are murdering some poor unfortunate travellers, thought I, and my time will come next. In about half an hour they returned, and threw something that fell like a dead heavy weight on the floor.

" By G——d we've done for him at last," said one; " the rascal fought like a tiger. Let's strip the gentleman of his hide."

" No, no," replied the other, " wait till—" here his voice sunk, and I could only guess at what was meant. I grew desperate, and tried to push up the window, but it was fastened down with nails, to make all sure, and prevent my escaping that way. I tried the trapdoor, but it turned out to be no trapdoor at all. I listened again, but by this time all was silent in the next room. The next moment I heard the voice of the old man calling his 'boys,' and perceived, to my astonishment, that the sun was just peeping above the eastern horizon. Daylight, which emboldens the innocent, appals the guilty, and I now felt myself safe. I came out of my room, with an air as unconcerned as possible, and was received as if nothing had happened.

"Good morning—good morning," said the impudent old republican, "I am afraid you was disturbed last night. The boys were out after a bear that has beat up our quarters several times. But he'll never come again I reckon. Isn't he a *whopper?*" continued he, pointing to the carcass in a corner. A happy turn, thought I, but I'm not to be humbugged by a cock-and-bull story. They pressed me to stay to breakfast, but I was resolved not to trust myself a moment longer with these banditti, and requested them to get my gig ready as soon as possible. In the mean time, I asked the old man for his bill.

"We don't keep a tavern," said he.

"I know that," replied I significantly, "but you will take something for your trouble?"

"Not a cent—every stranger that comes here is welcome to what I can offer. I have but little mo-

ney, but a plenty of every thing else, and it is not
often we have the pleasure of a stranger's company in this out-of-the-way place. You are heartily
welcome to your bed and supper, and will be still
more so, if you will stay to breakfast."

His refusal to take pay was another proof, if any
had been wanting, of the profession followed by
this awful family. Banditti are always above
taking money that is honestly their due, and require the zest of a little murder and bloodshed to
make it worth having. I bade them good morrow
with very little ceremony, and set off in a brisk
trot; but before I had got a quarter of a mile, I
heard some one hallooing, and looking back perceived one of the young giants, coming after
me in a pair of seven-leagued boots, as it appeared by his speed. I concluded they had re-
pented having spared my life, and had sent this
fine boy after, to despatch me. Under this impression I put my horse to his speed, and soon distanced the fellow, notwithstanding his seven-league
boots. I rode ten miles without stopping, being
determined to get out of the very atmosphere of
this nest of banditti, if possible.

By this time I was hungry, and conceiving myself pretty safe from any immediate pursuit, stopped at an inn of tolerable appearance. The landlord according to the custom of the country, took
the first opportunity to ask a few dozen questions,
ending with, "Pray what o'clock is it?" I told
him I didn't know, for I was resolved not to satis-

fy his impertinent curiosity. " O, ay," said he, " I see you hav'n't any watch." On examination I found this was but too true, and it at once occurred to my recollection that I had left it at the den of the banditti in the forest. I asked mine host if he knew these people, describing them and their establishment.

" What, old Hobby, that lives in the Pines, about ten miles off? Know him? Lord bless your heart, every body knows *him*."

I then condescended to tell him of my misfortune, and desired to know how I could get my watch again. He answered very shrewdly, that I had only to go back for it. But I would not have trusted myself there again for twenty watches. I told him I did not like the trouble of going back so far, but would pay any person reasonably that would ride over and get it for me. A bargain was struck with Pompey, the black boy, in which it was covenanted that the said Pompey, on returning with my watch, in the space of three hours, should receive from me a silver dollar for his pains. Pompey accordingly mounted a raw-boned courser—fastened a rusty spur to his bare heel— departed at full gallop, and returned with my watch in less than two hours and a half.

" Did they refuse the watch, Pompey?" said I.

" No!" replied Pompey with a grin.

" What did they say?"

" They said," replied Pompey, wonderfully

enlarging his grin, " that Massa was the drollest man they ever see in all their born days."

I felt no curiosity to inquire their reasons for this complimentary opinion, but paid Pompey his dollar, and said no more on the subject. After breakfast I sat out for Washington, where I arrived in safety, thanks to my good stars.

CHAP. XVII.

Washington—Dr. Thornton—Story of the roaring reprobate republican Ramsbottom—Story of an English emigrant farmer —His project—Disappointment. * * * * * * * * *

"Every thing is morally and physically mean at Washington," as the Quarterly says.* The breezes are perfumed by nuisances of all sorts— the flies die and mortify in the oily butter, and are eaten by the people as a great luxury†—drinking, dirking, and gouging, are the ordinary amusements—profanity and cheating the order of the day—the fire-flies and frogs furnish the lights and the music—the men are boisterous and rude—the children intolerable—the women all as ugly as sin —and to sum up all in one word, I was assured by Doctor Thornton, who saved the capital from being burnt last war—that "the whole country, like ancient Rome, is peopled by thieves and rob-

Vide No. 58, Eng. ed.   † Ibid.
18*

bers."* The Doctor told me in confidence that
although, like many other deluded Englishmen,
he had been induced to leave his country, yet he
was determined not one of his posterity should
take root after him in this detestable district.† The
Doctor presides over a department, where models
of machinery are deposited, and it furnishes another proof of the total ignorance of these immaculate republicans, that they were obliged to select
an Englishman for this station, because there was
not a single native in the whole country, that was
qualified for the place. The Doctor did not exactly say this, but he intimated as much. He
also further assured me that there was not a single
invention patented here, that he himself had not
previously anticipated. Yet these people pretend
to original genius.

To exemplify the state of manners and morals,
as well as the ferocious, intemperate passions engendered and fostered by the turbulent spirit of
democracy, the Doctor related to me the follow-

* Vide No. 58, Eng. ed.

† There is reason to suspect that the person here quoted, was
not the Dr. Thornton he professed himself to be, but an impos-
tor; or at any rate that the Doctor was bantering our Traveller
on these occasions. It is quite impossible he should have been
serious. There is the same unwarrantable freedom taken with
the name of this gentleman in Faux's Travels, as will be seen in
the 58th number of the Quarterly, (English ed.) to which our author so frequently refers. By the way people should be careful
how they attempt to *hoax* English travellers with these stories
for they will certainly record them as actual facts.—*Editor*.

'ing anecdote. The affair took place a few days before my arrival.

It seems a fellow by the name of Ramsbottom,[*]
a man-milliner by trade, and a roaring republican, had taken offence at a neighbour whose name
was Higginbottom, because his wife had attempted to cheapen a crimped tucker at his shop, and
afterwards reported that he sold his things much
dearer than his rival man-milliner who lived over
the way, whose name was Winterbottom, and
whose next door neighbour on the right hand was
named Leatherbottom, and on the left Oddy.   In
the pure spirit of democracy, Ramsbottom, who
was reckoned rather a good natured fellow for a
republican, determined to dirk not only Higginbottom, Winterbottom, Leatherbottom, and Oddy, but likewise their wives, together with all
the little Higginbottoms, Winterbottoms, Leatherbottoms, Oddys, and Oddities.   It was several
years before Ramsbottom could get them all together, so as to make one job of it.   At last, however, he collected the whole party at his own house,
which was next door to the Doctor's, to keep
their Christmas-eve, and determined to execute
his diabolical purpose.   It appears, however, that
he had previously changed his purpose of dirking, on account of the trouble, probably, as he

---

[*] Our author forgets that he has told this story before, two or
three times.   But this is excusable in a stranger.
                                        Printer's Devil.

was a lazy dog. Be this as it may, just as the whole party were up to their eyes in a Christmas pie, a horrible explosion took place—the house blew up, and every soul, Ramsbottom, Higginbottom, Winterbottom, Leatherbottom, their wives, and all the little innocent Ramsbottoms, Higginbottoms, Winterbottoms, Leatherbottoms, Oddys, and Oddities, were scattered in such minute and indivisible atoms, that not a vestige of them could be found the next day, except a little bit of Mrs. Higginbottom's fore finger, that was known by the length of the nail; it being the custom of the ladies of Washington to let that particular nail grow, for the purpose of protecting themselves against gouging at tea-parties and elsewhere. Such is the ferocity and deadly spirit of vengeance generated in the hotbed of polluted democracy, that the desperado, Ramsbottom, it appears, like another republican Samson of old, hesitated not to involve himself and all his family in destruction, only to be revenged upon a poor woman for cheapening a crimped tucker.

The first thing in Washington that excites the notice of a stranger who has been used to living under a monarchical, or what is the same thing, a christian dispensation, is, that there is not a single church in the whole city. This however is the case with every town and city in this country, founded since the revolution, when the turbulent spirit of democracy getting the upper hand, as

might be expected, the building of churches was
dispensed with, as highly aristocratic.   So much,
indeed, did the British troops feel the want of
some place of religious worship, when they entered the city during the late war, that as I was assured
by Dr. T——, the gallant Cockburn, actually delayed setting fire to the President's house a whole
hour, to afford them a decent place to say their
prayers.   The Doctor, solemnly declared to me,
it was the most' edifying sight he ever witnes-
sed, and that he looked upon the gallant Cockburn, as one of the genuine representatives of the
pious crusaders of yore, for he never went on a
burning or plundering expedition without saying
his prayers beforehand.

On Sunday morning (as it was, for the reason
before stated, impossible for me to attend church,)
it being excessively hot, I took my umbrella, and
strolled out into the solitudes of this immense
city.   I had not proceeded far, when I was assailed by a mob of some two or three hundred negroes and boys, who began pelting me with various
unseemly missiles.   Not knowing what offence
I had committed, I was in considerable perplexity, when a sober respectable person came up and
explained the whole matter.   "It is the custom
here," said he, "where but few persons enjoy
the luxury of hats, to put them on the top of their
umbrellas instead of their heads, in order to make
them the more conspicuous.   Your omitting to do
this, has caused a suspicion of your being an En-

glishman, and that you have not already lost both
eyes, a piece of your nose, and been roasted at a
log fire, is a great piece of good luck." By his
advice, I immediately did homage to the genius
of democracy, by placing my hat on the top of
my umbrella, and hoisting both over my head.
This appeased the mob, who gave three cheers,
under cover of which I retreated accompanied by
the stranger, who I at first took it for granted,
had a design to rob me, if not something worse.

Upon further intercourse and examination, however, I had a shrewd suspicion of his being one of
my own countrymen. He was a stout, square
built man, with a broad ruddy face, redolent of
small beer; all which appearances were in perfect
contrast with the rawboned, cadaverous figures of
the natives. Instead of the light loose pantaloons,
short gingham coats, and detestable straw hats, which
constitute the summer dress of the Yankee gentlemen, he wore a frock of genuine British broad-
cloth, a pair of corderoy breeches, and woollen
stockings, all which gave him a respectable and responsible appearance, although rather warm for the
season. These peculiarities, together with a certain
politeness of manner, and purity of language, almost
persuaded me that he was a true Englishman, and
presently afterwards, seeing him wipe his nose on
the sleeve of his coat, I became satisfied my con-
jectures were well founded. We soon became sociable, and continued our walk together some
time. I found him, like all the Englishmen I

have met with here, out of humour and discontented with every thing, the people, the country, the government, the air, the water, and most especially, the system of farming, and the obstinate ignorance of the American farmers.

"I brought with me to this country," said he, "rising of two thousand guineas, with part of which I bought a farm in Pennsylvania. Being determined to show them something in the way of farming, which they never saw before, for the honour of Old England, I sent home for iron ploughs, iron harrows, iron rakes, in short I had every thing of iron, even to my hog-trough. I also imported an English bull, English cows, English sheep, English hogs, an English dairy-woman, an English ploughman, English ploughs, and all sorts of English farming instruments. All this cost me a great deal of money—but I was determined to show the Yankee farmers something for the honour of Old England.

"As I expected huge crops owing to my improved system of English farming, I built large barns for my wheat and hay, large stables for my horses, oxen, cows, sheep, and other stock, for I was determined they should be well lodged. I spent a vast deal in hedging, ditching, and other improvements, the labour of which was rather expensive, and made another great hole in my guineas. However, I was resolved to show these bumpkins something in the way of farming, for the honour of Old England.

"I was so much taken up with these preparatory arrangements, that the season passed away before I had time to put in my crops, so that I was under the necessity of purchasing food and fodder for myself, and my English stock, which made another hole in my guineas. However, the spring came on, and I set to work, to show the Yankees something in the way of farming for the honour of Old England. My bull had been stuffed and currycombed till he had grown a perfect monster, so that when I turned him into the field, the neighbours came from ten miles round to see him. An old quaker, whose farm joined mine, said to me, 'Friend, I fear our earth is not strong enough for thy bull,' but I paid no attention to his slang.

"Being perfectly satisfied, from the analysis of Sir Humphrey Davy, that wheat, rye, corn, and the other grains cultivated in this country, contained little or no nourishment, compared with other products, I determined to put my whole force upon a field of four acres, which I devoted to the cultivation of *ruta baga*. With my iron plough, my iron harrow, and my English ploughman, assisted by two Yankee labourers, in the course of two months, I put my four acres into such order as never had been seen before. It was a perfect garden. The rows were as straight as arrows, and there was not a clod of earth above ground as large as an egg to be seen. Every body came to admire, but as yet nobody imitated me,—such is the ignorant and insolent obstinacy of the Yankee farmers. "Friend," said my neighbour, the old quaker—"friend Shortridge, what art thou going to put into thy field here?"

"Ruta baga."

"*Ruta baga!*—what is that, friend John?"

"Turnips," replied I.

"Well, why didn't thee call them so at first? If thou talkest Latin here, nobody will understand thee, friend John. But what art thou going to do with thy turnips?"

"I shall feed my cattle, sheep, and hogs with some, and sell the rest to my neighbours."

"But thy neighbours will raise their own turnips, and will not buy."

"Then I will send them to market."

"What, sixty miles, over a turnpike? That will be a bad speculation, friend John. Thee had best put in a few acres of wheat and corn, they will pay the expense of taking to market. Thy turnips will cost more than they will come to."

"Not I, indeed, friend Underhill," said I. "Sir Humphrey Davy says there is little or no nourishment in wheat and corn."

"No!" quoth the old quaker, with a sly glance at his round portly figure; "I have lived upon them all my life, and never made the discovery, friend John."

"My ruta baga flourished to the admiration of the whole neighbourhood, and when I came to gather my crop in the fall, there was a heap as high as a hay-stack. Some of them measured eighteen

19

inches in diameter.   I was as proud as a peacock,
for I had now done something for the honour of
old England.   I determined to give my cattle,
sheep, and hogs, a great feast, and invited my
good neighbour, the quaker, to see how they would
eat *ruta baga*.   A quantity was nicely cut up and
thrown to them one morning, but to my astonishment and mortification, not one would touch a
morsel.   Whether it was that they had become
spoiled by a fine season of grass, I cannot tell;
but the bull turned up his nose—the cows turned their backs, and so did the sheep, while the
pigs ran away screaming mightily.   ' Thee should
set them to reading Sir Humphrey Davy, friend
John,' quoth my neighbour—' they hav'n't learn
ing enough to relish thy Latin turnips.'

    " The autumn was now come, and there was a
long winter before me, for which, I confess, I was
but illy provided.   Relying on my *ruta baga*, I
had neglected my grass, or rather had pastured it
the whole season, depending on my turnips, as I
said before, for winter food for my stock.   I sent
a load of them to market, but the tolls and other
expenses swallowed up the price of the whole, and
brought me a little in debt.   I then offered to exchange ruta baga with my neighhours for hay and
other products, but they shook their heads and declined to a man.

    " On the back of this, came the loss of my fa-
mous bull, who one night got into a piece of low
ground, where he sunk in, and perished before

morning. ' I am sorry for thy loss friend John,
said the old quaker, ' but I told thee our earth was
not strong enough for a beast with such little short
legs, and such a huge body.' To mend the matter, my plump, rosy-faced, English dairy-maid
got married to a young fellow of the neighbourhood, whose father was a rich farmer, and my imported ploughman being told that a dram in the
morning was good for keeping off the ague and
fever, seemed to think he couldn't have too much
of a good thing, and was fuddled from morning
till night.

" Winter came on, and a terrible long hard winter was it. For some time I purchased what I
wanted for my family and stock of the neighbours,
but the spring turning out very backward, and the
frost continuing till late in April, all kinds of food
for cattle and stock became so scarce that there
was none to be had for love or money. As a last
resort, I resolved again to try the ruta baga. Accordingly, after preparing my cattle and pigs by a
long fast, I offered some to their acceptance. It was
Hopson's choice, and they nibbled a little, making
divers wry faces withal. By degrees they took
to it more kindly and ate freely. But somehow
or other, so far from thriving or growing fat upon
this fare, they dwindled away, so that many of them
gave up the ghost, and those that were turned to
pasture in the spring, looked like skeletons. The
old quaker came to look at them one day. ' Thy
cattle are rather lean, friend John,' said he, ' but

there is one comfort, they will not sink into the
marshes and perish, like thy fat Teeswater bull.'

"Thus ended my first season of farming. It
had not realized my expectations to be sure, but I
had now grown somewhat wiser by experience,
and was resolved this year to do something handsome for the honour of old England. About this
time my brother, a capital Norfolk farmer, wrote
me word Sir Humphrey Davy had just announced
to the world an analysis of carrots, by which it appeared they contained a greater quantity of saccharine matter than any other common vegetable, and
consequently more nourishment. Seizing this hint,
I turned my attention immediately to the cultivation of carrots, being resolved to reap the benefit
at once, before any body else entered into compe-
tition. I selected a field of sixteen acres, which
I employed six labourers to prepare and cultivate
under my direction. 'John,' said the old quaker,
'what art thou about this season? Art thou in love
with thy Latin turnips still?'

"Pshaw!" replied I, "carrots have twice as
much saccharine matter. I am going to cultivate
carrots."

"Friend John, thou wilt never prosper till thou
callest things by their honest christian names. But
what dost thou expect to do with thy sixteen acres
of carrots?"

"I shall feed my cattle with part, and send the
rest to market."

"Ah! John, John," exclaimed the old quaker, "remember thy turnips with the Latin name."

"My crop of carrots was amazing. I had such a quantity I did not know what to do with them, for my neighbours had enough of their own, and they were not worth taking to market. My cattle, to be sure, having little else, sometimes tried to eat them, but they some how or other, didn't thrive, and besides this, I and my family could not live upon carrots. This winter, therefore, I was again obliged to buy almost every thing I wanted, and the remainder of my guineas all vanished. Not only this, but I was compelled to take up money from the old quaker to a considerable amount, to buy stock to replace several of my horses, cows, and sheep, that died during the winter; for some how or other the saccharine matter of the carrots did not seem to agree with them. Every time I went to the quaker to borrow money, he would say, after letting me have it,—

Friend John, thee hadst better plant corn and sow wheat and rye, as we do, though they don't contain quite so much of the saccharine matter.' My reply usually was—' Friend Underhill, thy money is better than thy advice. I didn't come all the way from old England, to learn farming of you Yankees.

"But, although I put in practice regularly the most approved methods, recommended by Arthur Young, and other great English farmers, and adopt-

19*

ed every improvement I saw published, by the English agricultural societies, I as regularly went behind-
hand every year, and was obliged to borrow money, every now and then, of the old quaker, who
never failed to repeat his advice, which I always
treated in the same manner. Whoever heard of a
thorough-bred English farmer, demeaning himself
by imitating these ignorant Yankees?

"I had forgot to mention, among other instances, of the obstinacy with which these republicans
adhere to their barbarous notions, that they resist-
ed all my persuasions to adopt the wholesome
English custom of wearing woollen garments
during the summer. They stuck to their straw
hats and linen shirts and trowsers, and laughed at
my corduroy breeches and woollen stockings,
though I proved to them they were much the most
healthy and comfortable. To be sure I used to
perspire a little in the dog-days; but what of that?
I was resolved not to sacrifice the honour of old
England to the ignorance of these raw republicans.
The old quaker came to me one day, when the
thermometer was at ninety, and said in his sly
way—'Friend John, if thee is cold, I will lend
thee my great coat, for verily it is a bitter day,
for the season.' I took no notice of what he said,
for though I really did feel a little uncomfortable,
it would have been too great a triumph to these
people, to see me adopting any of their notions.

"At the end of three years I went one day to the
old quaker to take up some more money. 'Friend

John,' said he, ' hast thou ever read in Sir Humphrey Davy, or any of thine oracles, that borrowing day is always sooner or later followed by pay-
day? Thou hast been borrowing for the last three
years, without paying either principal or interest.
I cannot advance thee any more, for thy farm will
scarcely sell for what will pay the debt thou already owest me.' This was a thing that had not struck
me before, as I had never read of it either in Arthur Young or any other approved agriculturist. As
it was known all over the neighbourhood, **that**
my farm was mortgaged for its full value to the
quaker, my credit was now gone, and, in order to
raise money for the supply of my increasing wants,
I began to cut down the trees, and sell the timber
to the wheelwrights and others.

"Hearing of this the old quaker came to me
and said :—' Friend John, if thou goest on in this
way, thy farm will, by-and-by, be without wood,
and will not sell for wherewithal to pay my mort-
gages.   For thy sake, as well as mine, I shall fore-
close.' He did so ; my farm was sold at public
sale by the sheriff, and bought in by the old quaker to save himself from loss.   When I was on the
point of quitting the neighbourhood, he came to me
and said: 'Friend John, thou art going away
among strangers without money.   Here is fifty
dollars to begin the world again, which thou wilt
pay me when thou art able, and I will give thee a
little advice that will, if thou takest it, be worth
ten times as much.   It is, to remember whenever

thou comest into a strange country, there is always something to learn, as well as to teach. The
same shoe will not fit every body's foot, neither
will the same mode of farming suit every country.
The best farmer is not he that raises the greatest
crops, but he that raises them at the least expense.
In thy country, land is dear and labour cheap—in
ours, labour is dear and land cheap. This must
needs make a difference in the quantity of labour
which it is profitable to put on thy land, so that the
product will pay for thy labour. Moreover, thy
big bull with the little short legs, and thy big fat
sheep and cows, that can scarcely waddle along,
will do for the smooth lawns, close shaven hills,
and cool skies of thy country, but they will not
stand our hot summers, our swampy low grounds
and our rough rocky mountains. Moreover, I do
most specially recommend thee to eschew turnips
with Latin names;—to plant corn and potatoes, sow
wheat and rye, like thy neighbours, and, above
all, abjure Sir Humphrey Davy and his saccharine
matter. Farewell, friend John, I wish thee better success another time.' "

I have given this story as nearly as possible for
the purpose of exhibiting at full length a warning
example to our English farmers at home, who may
be about to emigrate to this country. In order to
succeed, they must, in the first place, accommodate themselves to situation and circumstances,
which is contrary to the independent nature and
feelings of a true-born Englishman. Instead of

the soil, climate, products, and seasons accommo-
dating themselves to their mode of farming, as
they ought to do, considering its immense superiority, our farmers, forsooth, must pay homage to
the genius of democracy, and degrade themselves
by stooping to learn where they came to teach.
They must consent to grow articles that will pay
for carrying to market, although they don't contain half the quantity of saccharine matter which
others do—they must plant corn and wheat, instead of carrots and ruta baga—they must unlearn
their own knowledge, and adopt the ignorance of
others—they must even consult the wayward appetites of their imported cattle and pigs, who seem
actually to become sophisticated, by breathing the
air of democracy, and occasionally smelling to the
Yankee cattle over a stone wall.

After spending the whole morning together,
strolling along the shady river, we returned to dinner. The day was so excessively hot, that I almost caught myself envying the Yankees their
straw hats, gingham short coats, and linen pantaloons. My poor friend in the woollen stockings,
panted like a tired mastiff, and perspired like an
ox; but still there was something very respectable
in his blue broad-cloth frock, striped swansdown
waistcoat, corduroy breeches, and gray woollen
hose. I forgot to mention that this deluded, though
worthy man, had come to Washington for the purpose of petitioning the congress to establish a farm
at the public expense, and under his special direc-

tion, in the view of giving a practical illustration of the benefits of a system of farming adapted to an old country, when applied to a new one. But his proposal was treated with the most stupid indifference by the arrogant, self-sufficient, bundling, gouging, guessing, drinking, dirking, spitting, chewing, pig-stealing, impious genius of democracy, as the Quarterly says. * * * * *

THE END.